THE
NEW YORK
OBELISK

or
How Cleopatra's
Needle Came
to New York
and
What Happened
When
It Got Here

Martina D'Alton

The Metropolitan Museum of Art/Abrams

On February 22, 1881, a truly monumental occasion took place in the grand hall of the Metropolitan Museum, the formal presentation of the gift of Cleopatra's Needle to the City of New York from the government of Egypt. A committee headed by founding trustee and Commissioner of Public Parks Henry G. Stebbins and the Museum's first president, John Taylor Johnston, sensed extraordinary public interest in this monolith, which had been making its way across Manhattan for the past four months, and issued tickets of admission. But the crowds surged: early arrivals packed the steps and lines stretched in all directions, blocking stairways and sidewalks. The crush was reported by the *New York World* to be like a "favorite opera night ten times intensified." However, it was "an amiable throng" that soon settled down, content to look through the windows at the "towering shaft . . . clear cut against a cloudless sky."

Johnston presided over the ceremonies, which took place almost precisely a year after the dedication of the Museum's first permanent home in Central Park, a red-brick neo-Gothic structure designed by Calvert Vaux and Jacob Wrey Mould. After a prayer and a hymn, Stebbins's introductory address was read to the audience, as a "severe cold" prevented his attendance. This "artistic memorial," he wrote of the obelisk, "now fitly looks on the beginning of what I trust will become a great museum of art. . . . I hope that the successful placing of this interesting monument in relation to the future national gallery of America will encourage our wealthy citizens to enlarge the Art Museum and to fill it with all those treasures which so greatly increase the attractions of the metropolis." His words turned out to be prophetic, and among the first Egyptian objects donated to the Museum that very year were two of the bronze crabs placed by the Romans at the base of the obelisk, a gift of the transporter of the monolith, H. H. Gorringe. These were followed by increasing numbers of donations of Egyptian art, and by 1911, the collection had grown in size to ten galleries of objects from almost every important era of Egyptian civilization. As Stebbins saw it, Cleopatra's Needle, standing as it were in "a great outdoor gallery," would be a harmonious extension of this flourishing museum.

Last year The Metropolitan Museum of Art reaped a most unusual benefit from its relationship with Cleopatra's Needle: in November we opened our new Trustees Dining Room, whose splendid view boasts the obelisk as its dramatic center point. This publication, adapted by writer and editor Martina D'Alton from Gorringe's fascinating account of the acquisition, importation, and reraising of the obelisk, is part documentary and part celebratory; for we are indeed fortunate to have this "graceful and suggestive monument," to use Stebbins's words, so superbly and agreeably located in such proximity to the Museum.

Philippe de Montebello
Director

Library of Congress Cataloging-in-Publication Data

D'Alton, Martina.
  The New York obelisk, or, How Cleopatra's Needle came to New York and what happened when it got here / Martina D'Alton.
    p. cm.
    ISBN 0-87099-680-0.—ISBN 0-8109-6425-2 (Abrams)
    1. Cleopatra's Needle (New York, N.Y.) 2. New York (N.Y.)—Buildings, structures, etc. I. Metropolitan Museum of Art (New York, N.Y.) II. Title. III. Title: New York obelisk. IV. Title: How Cleopatra's Needle came to New York and what happened when it got here.
F128.64.C57D35   1993
974.7'1—dc20   93-1803
                                           CIP

Above: A card from the 1880s celebrating the arrival of Cleopatra's Needle in New York.

Prologue

*"They called them obelisks and
dedicated them to the Sun-god."*

Pliny the Elder
Natural History

Around thirty-five hundred years ago, a crew of Egyptian stonecutters was sent to the dry and dusty quarries at Aswan. It was the reign of Thutmosis III, a great warrior-king and strategist, the Napoleon of Eighteenth-Dynasty Egypt. Even empire building had its off season, however, and every winter when the rains threatened, Thutmosis turned his armies homeward to Egypt. There his restless energy and full treasuries meant the building of new temples, palaces, and monuments, strung like jewels along the Nile.

As pharaoh, Thutmosis celebrated at least three jubilees, marking each by raising a pair of obelisks in front of one of Egypt's magnificent temples. The stonecutters' mission at Aswan was to detach two huge blocks of richly colored pink granite that would be turned into obelisks for their pharaoh's third jubilee, held about 1443 B.C. Just how the quarrymen accomplished their task is not known for certain, but there are clues in the walls and rubble of the quarry, in a few texts, and, especially, in the ancient engineers' failures.

The Unfinished Obelisk of Aswan, for example, had been freed on all but one side, yet after months of back-breaking work, it was aban-doned in its bed with cracks and fissures that defied correction. It may date to the time of Queen Hatshepsut (r. 1473–1458 B.C.), Thutmosis's step-mother, and at 133 feet long, it would have been the tallest obelisk in Egypt had it been completed. Instead, the stone was left "sleeping in the desert," as Amelia Edwards described it in her 1877 travel book. Indeed, over the millennia sand had partially buried the shaft, and Egyptologists were not able to study it carefully until 1922 when it was excavated by Reginald Engelbach, an English archaeologist and the chief inspector of antiquities for Upper Egypt.

Engelbach's observations at Aswan led him to reject many previous theories about how obelisks were formed. Instead of wedging or chiseling the monoliths loose, as had been suggested, work crews probably used balls of dolerite, a tough rock found in Egypt's Eastern Desert and known for its crushing strength. Dozens of these small balls, each weighing up to twelve pounds, littered the surrounding quarry. The workers most likely held the dolerite in their hands and pounded against the surface, pulverizing the granite.

Thutmosis III (r. 1479–1425 B.C.) may be best remembered for his triumphant military campaigns in the Near East, but he was also the original owner of New York's obelisk. (Fragmentary relief. Purchase, Edward S. Harkness Gift, 1926. 26.7.1399)

3

The Unfinished Obelisk at Aswan, ca. 1966. The Aswan quarries and their haunted quality fascinated travelers in the nineteenth century. Vivant Denon, Napoleon's observer in Egypt, found marks left in the stone by ancient workers to be "so fresh in the unalterable material that to look at them one would suspect that the work had been interrupted only yesterday."

The first challenge facing the quarrymen would have been selecting a suitable site in the quarry. This must have been a nerve-wracking decision for Yamu-nedjeh, Thutmosis's First Herald, who had been sent to supervise the project. Test holes, each about a yard square, were laboriously sunk to search out flaws in the stone. Despite such precautions, however, costly mistakes were sometimes made, as the Unfinished Obelisk dramatically demonstrates.

If all went well the quarrymen would pound out trenches along the lengths of the future obelisks. The scores of men working on Thutmosis's monuments may have sung to maintain the rhythm of their work. "With a good chanter," observed Engelbach in the 1920s, "who can extemporise rhyming lines full of highly flavoured personalities, the work the Egyptians can do is little short of marvelous." Archaeologists excavating just after World War II recall that when a crew ran out of rhyming lyrics they chanted ancient phrases, which had since lost their meaning. Some said that the words originated in old Egypt, among laborers such as those who worked in the pharaohs' quarries and building sites.

As the trenches around the obelisks deepened, overseers inspected the stone for horizontal cracks not visible on the top surface. Once the quarrymen had completed the trenches, they pounded through the granite underneath to free each block completely from the parent rock. As rubble was removed, heavy beams of wood or blocks of stone were slid in place to support the weight of the emerging obelisks.

Ancient writers, such as Pliny the Elder (A.D. 23–79), who devoted part of his *Natural History* (36:14) to obelisks, gloss over the details of removal and transportation, and no Egyptian texts yet known illuminate the specifics fully, but again there are some clues to the process. A painting in the tomb of Djehuti-hotep, a Twelfth-Dynasty governor, for example, depicts a colossal statue on a sledge being dragged by 172 men. Hard labor like this may have cost many lives. An expedition to bring large blocks of stone from the Eastern Desert for Ramesses IV apparently caused the loss of 900 men out of 8,368.

Thutmosis's two obelisks were probably levered from the quarry floor onto huge sledges, which were then dragged along an embankment to the Nile to await the spring floods that would make it possible to load them onto a barge. They may have traveled on separate vessels or together on a single one, as had obelisks belonging to Queen Hatshepsut. The two shafts honoring the queen were loaded end to end on a mammoth barge,

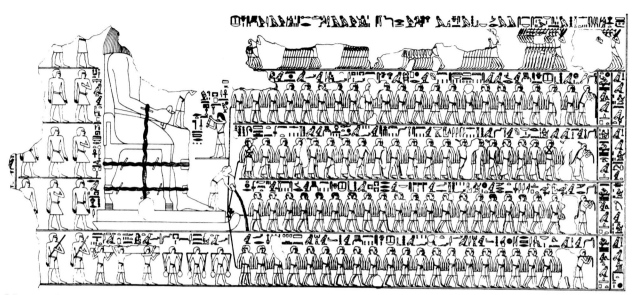

Moving the monumental statue of Djehuti-hotep. A similar method may have been used to move obelisks. This drawing was made by Howard Carter in about 1908 from a wall relief at el-Bersheh.

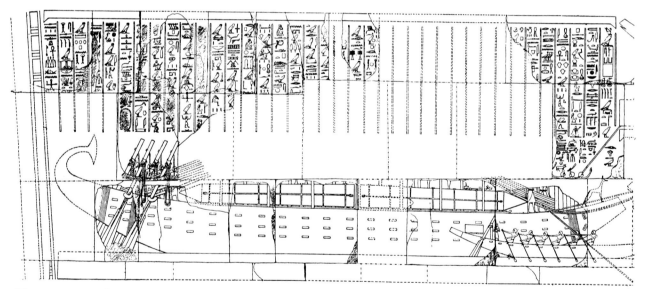

The enormous barge used to transport two of Queen Hatshepsut's obelisks was drawn from a wall relief during Edouard Naville's 1906/7 season of work in Hatshepsut's temple at Deir al-Bahari.

which was towed down the Nile by thirty smaller boats. In any case, whether on two vessels or one, Thutmosis's monoliths began their journey from Aswan together, although their travels would end separately, thousands of years later, with one in London and the other in New York.

After the trip down the Nile, the stones reached their first stop, the sacred city of On, which the Greeks called Heliopolis. Records found in the tomb of Yamu-nedjeh tell us that both obelisks were raised with great ceremony before the Temple of the Sun, one on each side of the portal.

The solitary obelisk of Senwosret I (r. 1971–1926 B.C.) is almost all that remains of ancient Heliopolis, now a suburb of modern Cairo. In the nineteenth century, when German archaeologist Richard Lepsius stopped to study the obelisk, he found a garden growing around it. "The flowers of the garden," he wrote, "have attracted a quantity of bees, and these could find no more commodious lodging than in the deep and sharply cut hieroglyphics of the obelisk."

Raising an obelisk was a difficult undertaking, as risky as quarrying the stone, and the pharaoh himself was probably present to witness it. Pliny recounts that when one of Ramesses's obelisks, an unusually large one, was about to be raised, the pharaoh grew anxious. To impress upon the workers the need for care, he "tied his son to the pinnacle, intending that the stone should share the benefit of his deliverance at the hands of the laborers." Clumsy handling or faulty equipment would have meant the loss of the boy along with the obelisk. Engelbach points out, however, that the story, if true, is to be taken with a grain of salt. If the pharaoh named was Ramesses II, he could probably afford to risk a son because he was known to have had at least one hundred.

The two obelisks of Thutmosis III stayed in place for about fifteen hundred years. Within the first two centuries, Ramesses II (r. 1279–1212 B.C.) had added two vertical lines of flowery self-serving inscriptions on each face of the obelisks to flank those of Thutmosis III. (Ramesses made it a practice, space allowing, to add his name to those on earlier monuments.) About 920 B.C., although the obelisks were by now overcrowded with inscriptions, another pharaoh, Osorkon I of the Twenty-first Dynasty, managed to squeeze his own name on the lower edges.

Several centuries after Osorkon's reign, in 525 B.C., when Egypt's decline as a world power was almost complete, the two obelisks survived the storming and torching of Heliopolis by the Persian conquerer Cambyses. Pliny tells us that Cambyses was so impressed by the city's obelisks that he ordered the fires put out before they reached them. His account is wrong, however; later evidence proved that Thutmosis's pair of obelisks had been toppled and burned.

Another five hundred years or so passed before the obelisks began their second journey. By then, the Romans had turned Egypt into a corner of their empire. Awed by Egypt's magnificent past, but not content simply to admire it, the Romans began to move things about and even add a monument or two, such as the Temple of Dendur in Nubia (brought to the Metropolitan Museum in 1968). It was built during the reign of Augustus Caesar, who also ordered Thutmosis's two obelisks to be floated down the Nile from Heliopolis to Alexandria in about 12 or 10 B.C.

The Romans seem to have had a special liking for obelisks. Augustus and the other Caesars uprooted many of them and brought them to Rome, where one, now called the Monte Citorio obelisk, is known to have been used as a somewhat unreliable sundial. Even the monumental ships the Romans built to carry their treasured monoliths across the Mediterranean were greatly admired. Pliny writes that one of these was "preserved for many years by Claudius of Revered Memory," as deceased and deified Caesars came to be called, "for it was the most amazing thing that had ever been seen at sea."

The next chapter in the tale of this ship is told by the historian Suetonius (born A.D. 70). He writes in his history of the twelve Caesars that when Claudius, who was emperor from A.D. 41 to 54, constructed a new breakwater at Ostia, he "used the ship in which Caligula had transported a great obelisk from Heliopolis; it was first sunk then secured with piles and finally crowned with a very tall lighthouse, like the Pharos at Alexandria." The story of this ship does not end there. Its ruins were uncovered not long ago by construction workers at Rome's Fiumicino Airport. The obelisk it carried may be the one standing outside Saint Peter's at the Vatican. As for Rome's other obelisks, it is difficult to turn a corner in the heart of the city today without bumping into one of the thirteen still standing.

Although Augustus may have intended eventually to bring Thutmosis's two obelisks to Rome, he first had them raised in Alexandria in front of the Caesarium, the temple to the deified Julius Caesar, and there they remained. Bronze supports in the form of sea crabs (perhaps associated with the Roman sun god), were placed under the corners, which had broken off.

Also around this time the pair may have acquired the well-known nickname Cleopatra's Needles. Its origin is uncertain, but it is probably a fanciful attribution more than anything else, as Cleopatra died some twenty years before the obelisks arrived in Alexandria. We do know that in the late twelfth century an Arab doctor named Abd al-Latif, who traveled in Egypt, wrote about them as "Cleopatra's big needles."

The Lateran obelisk, originally at Karnak, was probably the last to be raised by Thutmosis III, and at a height of over 105 feet is the largest now surviving. In the fourth century A.D. it was moved from Egypt to Rome and raised in the Circus Maximus. Some time later, it toppled over and was buried. In the sixteenth century Pope Sixtus V had his agents probe among the ruins until they found it some twenty-three feet underground. It was excavated and raised in the Piazza di San Giovanni in Laterno in 1588.

In Alexandria Thutmosis's pair of obelisks quietly faded into the scenery, their presence taken for granted by the Alexandrians. The Roman empire collapsed. The sea gradually swamped and eventually swallowed much of the Caesarium and other nearby buildings along the shifting shoreline. The obelisks remained unperturbed, however, greeting incoming ships and witnessing the

The obelisk of Ramesses II now in Paris was paired with another that still stands outside the Temple of Luxor. Its removal to Paris, initiated in 1831, was beset by difficulties and delays and took French engineers more than five years to complete.

departure of obelisks and other treasures bound for distant shores. Then, about 1301, a catastrophic earthquake struck Alexandria and its environs and one of the obelisks toppled, although it was fortuitously unbroken.

By the dawn of the nineteenth century Napoleon's army had bivouacked nearby and Vivant Denon, who was making a study of Egypt's monuments for the emperor, had sketched the two obelisks, noting that "they might both be conveyed to France without difficulty, and would there become a trophy of conquest, and a very characteristic one, as they are themselves a monument."

The French army did not last long in Egypt, but the interest their occupation aroused throughout the Western world sparked a century of rediscovery. A steady stream of artists, photographers, fledgling archaeologists and Egyptologists, and travelers on the grand tour stopped to gaze at Alexandria's obelisks. In 1867 Samuel Clemens shepherded a group he called "the lost tribes of America" on a tour of Europe, the Holy Land, and Egypt. His amusing letters home, first published in newspapers, were gathered into his liveliest travel book: *The Innocents Abroad; or The New Pilgrims' Progress* (1869).

He took his troupe of travelers to see the sights in Alexandria where, as he writes, "they went in picturesque procession to the American Consul's; to Cleopatra's Needles; to Pompey's Pillar; to the palace of the Viceroy of Egypt; to the Nile; to the superb groves of date palms. One of our most inveterate relic-hunters had his hammer with him, and tried to break a fragment off the upright Needle and could not do it; he tried the prostrate one and failed; he borrowed a heavy sledge hammer from a mason and failed again."

Other souvenir hunters were more successful, returning home with chunks of stone and other mementos from their trips to Egypt. In 1833 a French monk, Father Geramb, had explained to Mohammed Ali Pasha, the viceroy of Egypt, "It would be hardly respectable, on one's return from Egypt, to present oneself in Europe without a mummy in one hand and a crocodile in the other." In those days there was no Egyptian Antiquities Service controlling permits and concessions.

With a touch of longing for the permissiveness of that earlier time, Howard Carter, the archaeologist who cleared Tutankhamun's tomb in 1922, describes the early part of the nineteenth century as "the great days of excavating. Anything to which a fancy was taken, from a scarab

The remaining obelisk of Ramesses II at Luxor. A mosque built within the temple is viewed through the portal.

to an obelisk, was just appropriated." And so in 1831 the French plucked one of Ramesses II's obelisks from the temple at Luxor and raised it in Paris five years later.

Not to be outdone, the English laid claim to their own prize. They had been given the fallen Alexandrian obelisk in 1801 by a grateful Egyptian government for their role in ousting Napoleon's occupation army. The gift was con-

firmed by Mohammed Ali Pasha in 1820, but it was not until 1877 that the English actually took possession. They built a kind of cigar-tube vessel around it, rolled it into the Mediterranean, and towed it toward England. After a hazardous journey that took the lives of several members of the crew, it was raised in London in 1878.

That same year Ulysses S. Grant and General William T. Sherman were escorted up the

The obelisk of Thutmosis III, London. Raised on the Thames Embankment on September 13, 1878, the London obelisk is the mate to Cleopatra's Needle in New York.

Nile by Consul-General Elbert E. Farman, who would play a key role in negotiating for Cleopatra's other needle. Not surprisingly, the standing obelisk was the first stop on their itinerary. Also around this time a U.S. Navy engineer, Lieutenant-Commander Henry Honeychurch Gorringe, soon to figure prominently in the story of the New York obelisk, was conducting a hydrographic survey of the Mediterranean.

Gorringe was born in Barbados in 1840, the son of an Oxford-trained Swedish missionary. At the age of fourteen, over his father's objections, he had gone to sea as a cabin boy. Among his adventures as a youngster, on a single voyage he survived a storm rounding the Cape of Good Hope and then was shipwrecked on a desolate stretch of Indian coastline. A kindly missionary in India arranged for his passage to America, and in 1862 Gorringe joined the U.S. Navy, serving during the Civil War with the Union's Mississippi Squadron. In 1868 he was made a lieutenant-commander and stationed in New York City. In 1872 he was transferred to the Hydrographic Office in Washington, D.C., where he spent the next four years.

Gorringe loved the life at sea, however, and grew restless behind a desk. In 1876 he was given command of the *Gettysburg*, a tired old paddle-wheel blockade runner that had been captured from the Confederates during the Civil War. Although refitted and recommissioned, it was fraught with mechanical and structural problems. Even so, Gorringe and Lieutenant Seaton Schroeder, a fellow officer at the Hydrographic Office, were happy to be at sea in any vessel, steaming toward the Mediterranean where their mission was to update existing charts and draw up new ones for the coasts and islands. En route they tested equipment for taking depth measurements, and with it snagged the top of a submerged mountain in the Atlantic Ocean. Presumed to be proof of "lost Atlantis," it was located near the Azores on what came to be called Gorringe Bank. President Grant, then in his last year in office, sent Gorringe a congratulatory telegram for his discovery.

During the course of the two-year survey, the *Gettysburg* broke down and limped into Alexandria for repairs. It was then that Gorringe first saw Cleopatra's Needle, standing alone since the departure of the fallen obelisk. Schroeder recalls in his memoirs, written some forty years later, that the two men "occasionally visited the obelisk which stood there, and commented upon its unattractive surroundings and its utter loneliness. But I did not know, though I might have suspected, that in Captain Gorringe's restless mind had arisen vaguely the question as to how he would do it if it came to him to take it to America."

A year or so later, in 1879, Gorringe would have the opportunity to answer that question and put his plans into action, transporting Cleopatra's Needle to New York. Its arrival here was not a minute too soon according to some, if the city's reputation was to be preserved. In 1881 a reporter for the *New York Herald* wrote, "it would be absurd for the people of any great city to hope to be happy without an Egyptian Obelisk. Rome has had them this great while and so has Constantinople. Paris has one. London has one. If New York was without one, all those great sites might point the finger of scorn at us and intimate that we could never rise to any real moral grandeur until we had our obelisk."

Gorringe gives a most dignified account of his adventures in *Egyptian Obelisks*, which he published privately in 1882. The quoted text that follows, unless otherwise noted, is taken from his book. Many of the photographs in his book are also reproduced here. They were largely taken by Edward Bierstadt, brother of Albert Bierstadt, the renowned landscape painter of the American West.

We are also indebted to a dedicated scrapbook compiler, who, beginning in 1879, clipped and pasted newspaper reports, magazine articles, engravings, trade cards, photographs, and other memorabilia pertaining to the story of how Cleopatra's Needle came to America. Much of the material is included here. The presence of an invitation inscribed to "Mr. Davis" makes it

Henry Honeychurch Gorringe (1841–1885)

tempting to identify the scrapbook's original owner as Theodore M. Davis, a wealthy New York attorney and amateur Egyptologist who held the concession for digging in the Valley of the Kings from 1902 to 1914. However, Davis is a common name—a "Mr. Davis" was also the chief carpenter for the obelisk project—and the true identity of the scrapbook's owner may never be known.

1. The Gift

"We happened to meet near a settee and the Khedive invited me to be seated. His first words were: 'Well, Mr. Farman, you would like an obelisk.'"

The Century
May–October 1882

In 1849 Gustave Flaubert, about to embark on a trip up the Nile, had called Alexandria "almost a European city, there are so many Europeans here." By 1880 the foreign population had increased still further, and the city was growing at a rapid pace. The obelisk, once prominent on the shoreline, was being engulfed by urban sprawl.

"The standing obelisk of Alexandria," writes Gorringe, "was generally the first and the last of Egypt's numerous monuments to be visited by travellers. [Yet a] feeling of disgust [was] aroused by some of its surroundings. Something more than curiosity was needed to induce one to approach near enough and remain long enough to examine and appreciate it. Situated in the outskirts of the city, near the Ramleh railway depot, it was a familiar object to the foreign element, many of whom live at Ramleh and pass it twice, often four times a day; and yet no one deemed it worthy of protection and care, even to the extent of preventing its defacement and the accumulation of offal around it. Two men made a business of breaking pieces from the angle of the shaft and edges of the intaglios for sale to relic hunters. The disagreeable odors and clamors for backsheesh hastened the departure of strangers, who rarely devoted more than a few seconds to its examination. . . .

"The first suggestion [for] the removal of an obelisk from Egypt to the United States was made by His Highness, Ismaïl, the Khedive of Egypt, at the time of the opening of the Suez Canal in 1869, to Mr. William Henry Hurlbert [editor of the *New York World*]."

This was a feverish period in Egyptian history. Egypt was caught in the push and pull of other nations, and both England and France vied for control of the government and thus of the newly built canal. The khedive, Ismail Pasha, who was obsessed with building projects, had pushed Egypt to the brink of bankruptcy to finance his extravagant schemes. He had reached deep into the treas-

The announcement of Egypt's gift caused great excitement in New York. In a cartoonist's vision in *The Daily Graphic* (July 30, 1880) a would-be welcoming committee includes William H. Vanderbilt and William Henry Hurlbert, holding a copy of his paper, the *New York World*. Hurlbert took credit for suggesting the gift to the khedive.

Ismail Pasha (1830–1895). At the opening of the Suez Canal, the khedive told Hurlbert that "he had been struck by the absence of the American flag from the great parade of ships of all nations through the Suez canal and he was firmly convinced that the prosperity of Egypt would be advanced by... whatever he could do to bring Egypt and America more closely together" (*Harper's Weekly*, July 3, 1880). Cleopatra's Needle made an impressive token of friendship.

Tawfiq Pasha (1852–1892). "There has been all sort of pressure upon me to retain the obelisk," the prince told a newspaper reporter. "But I assure you it will give me great pleasure to hear of this obelisk being erected in America, where, I hope, it will not only create interest there in the ancient Egyptian monuments, but, by awakening general inquiry as to Egypt, may possibly lead to the [establishment] of trade between the United States and Egypt" (*New York Herald*, November 3, 1879).

uries and had taxed and swindled many of his subjects out of their land, possessions, and even their freedom, for the canal and other projects were built with slave labor. He had used Egypt's antiquities both to raise capital and to buy influence. The gift of an obelisk to the United States might mean new backers for his plans to modernize Egypt.

By 1877 Henry Hurlbert, who was spearheading the project to bring the obelisk to New York, had interested John Dixon, an English civil engineer, in participating. Dixon was then at work moving the fallen obelisk to London. Hurlbert had also enlisted the financial backing of William Henry Vanderbilt and the political support of Henry G. Stebbins, New York's com-

missioner of public parks. By this time, however, the khedive seemed to be having second thoughts about the gift, perhaps under pressure by nationalist forces to protect Egypt's treasures. When Dixon's efforts to obtain the khedive's permission to remove the obelisk came to nothing, Stebbins petitioned the secretary of state to intervene. He in turn instructed the American consul-general in Egypt, Elbert Farman, to use his persuasive powers with the khedive to secure Cleopatra's Needle for America.

"The secretary's dispatch was a great surprise to me," wrote Farman in *The Century*. But on March 4, 1878, Farman "obtained an interview with the Khedive at the Palace of Abdin.... He said that, while it would be a great pleasure

Bonfils.

17. Alexandrie, Obelisque de Cleopâti

Cleopatra's Needle rises above its humble surroundings in Alexandria. Gorringe called it "impossible for anything to have been more neglected and less appreciated than was the Alexandrian obelisk by the residents of Alexandria and tourists who passed through the city en route to the Nile." This photograph, taken by Felix Bonfils, probably dates to about 1878.

for him to accede to my wishes, as to the obelisk at Alexandria, he did not think it best even to mention it, since the people of that city would make too much opposition to its removal."

Over the next year, Farman continued to press the khedive gently whenever they met. It was at a dinner party that "the first favorable in-timation was given in regard to the obelisk," writes Farman. The khedive "seemed in better spirits than was usual. . . . We happened to meet near a settee, and he invited me to be seated. His first words were: 'Well, Mr. Farman, you would like an obelisk.'"

Farman's goal was not to be achieved quite

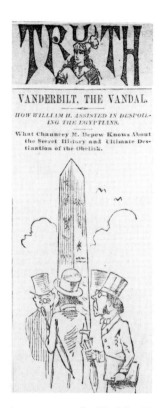

VANDERBILT, THE VANDAL.

*HOW WILLIAM H. ASSISTED IN DESPOIL-
ING THE EGYPTIANS.*

What Chauncey M. Depew Knows About
the Secret History and Ultimate Destination of the Obelisk.

Not all Americans were thrilled by Egypt's gift. According to the *Evening Telegram* (November 6, 1879), "a petition remonstrating against the removal of Cleopatra's Needle is being circulated and has received numerous influential signatures." The *New York Sun* (October 31, 1879) joined the opposition and labeled the obelisk "terrific humbug. It has no beauty and no shapeliness. It is only a broken, decayed and disfigured old block of stone." Such carping was soon lost in the swell of enthusiasm for the impending arrival of Cleopatra's Needle.

so easily, however. "Turns of the wheel of fortune are not only frequent in Egypt," he continues, "but they generally happen when least expected. It is called a country of surprises and there is an Oriental proverb according to which only provisional things are permanent." The khedive was beset with difficulties caused by famine, debt, and political rivals and was threatened with a coup d'état and even open revolution. When it seemed certain that Ismail's days in power were numbered, Farman made a special plea for confirmation of the gift. In a letter dated May 18, 1879, the khedive's agent wrote, "The Govern-

ment of the Khedive having taken into consideration your representations, and the desire which you have expressed in the name of the Government of the United States of America, consent, in fact to make a gift to the city of New York of the obelisk known as Cleopatra's Needle, which is at Alexandria on the sea-shore."

Farman had maneuvered through a maze of foreign objections and political intrigue, of attempted coups and countercoups, of local rivalries, and the stirrings of Egyptian nationalism. A month after the gift was formalized, the khedive abdicated in favor of his son Tawfiq Pasha. Only the existence of the written agreement secured by Farman prevented the new ministry from rescinding the gift. The need for careful timing that had plagued the negotiations would also be a factor in the removal process.

William Henry Vanderbilt (1827–1885). As the project's backer, Vanderbilt made an easy target for the opposition.

2. The Plan

"Its size was as embarrassing as its weight...."

Cleopatra's Needle measures just over sixty-nine feet from base to tip; at the base it is almost eight feet across. It weighs anywhere from 193 to about 220 tons. The pedestal and steps, which traveled with the obelisk from Alexandria, together are about twenty-seven feet high. The pedestal alone weighs 50 tons. Any plan to transport such a load would have to include not only an especially seaworthy ship in which to cross the Atlantic but also a method of lowering the obelisk in Alexandria, moving it through the city, loading it onto the ship, unloading it again in New York, transporting it to its new site, and raising it again. It was a formidable challenge to an engineer.

Gorringe had studied earlier removals and had determined to improve upon them, particularly in the choice of a ship. The vessels used by the French and English to carry their obelisks were unsuited to a transatlantic voyage. Gorringe's experience as a mariner told him "that the vessel in which the New York obelisk was to be transported must be large enough to take care of herself under all conditions of weather, and must have her own motive power. . . . [As for the obelisk,] its size was as embarrassing as its weight. No vessel has hatches that will admit a mass sixty-nine feet in length. It could not have been carried on deck in safety without strengthening the vessel at great expense. In the hold, below the water-line, was the only place where it could be securely stowed and safely transported, and how to get it there was the one thing on which the whole operation of removing it successfully turned.

"The plan devised and successfully executed consisted simply in embarking and disembarking the obelisk while the bow of the vessel was out of water, through an aperture opened expressly for the purpose and subsequently closed for the voyage."

For pivoting the obelisk, Gorringe designed a turning structure that would be made in pieces, shipped to Alexandria, assembled, and put into action. It would then be taken apart and would travel back to New York with the obelisk to be used in installing it there. Because none of the literature agreed on the exact dimensions of Cleopatra's Needle, the design had to accommodate a range of possibilities.

"For lowering the obelisk to the ground after it was horizontal," writes Gorringe, "two plans were devised, and the selection left to circumstances. One was by means of an inclined plane, the other by means of hydraulic pumps placed on stacks of timber built up under the ends. . . .

"There remained only the land transport of the obelisk to provide for to complete my plans for its removal from Alexandria. For this there were abundant precedents successfully applied in ancient and modern times. Of these the most ingenious is the method devised by Count Carburi . . . to move the pedestal of the statue of Peter the Great from the forest of Keralia to St. Petersburg. . . . The essential feature of Carburi's plan was the substitution of cannon-balls for the ordinary wheels or rollers and metal grooves for the ordinary tracks."

Gorringe's proposal was accepted by Hurlbert and Vanderbilt over those submitted by three other applicants. Each of the alternatives dealt only with the obelisk's removal. In the first, proposed

Scenes carved on the pedestal of Thutmosis III's obelisk in Istanbul, where it was moved in the fourth century A.D. In the top two rows teams of men turn capstans to drag the obelisk forward. The bottom row may depict activities in the Hippodrome after the obelisk's installation. This engraving, first published in 1678, combines reliefs on the north and south sides of the pedestal.

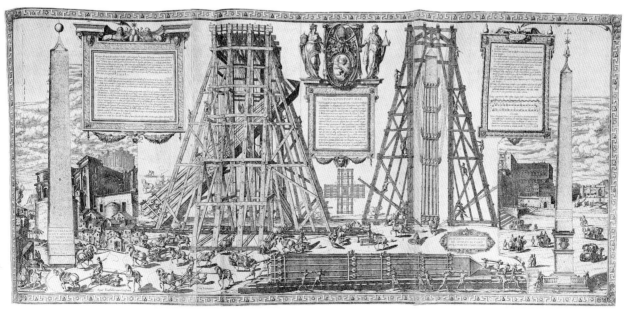

Among the precedents studied by Gorringe was Domenico Fontana's 1586 plan for moving the Vatican obelisk from beside Old Saint Peter's to Saint Peter's Square, depicted in a contemporary engraving. Most of the work was accomplished by men turning capstans. (Natale Bonifacio after Giovanni Guerra, 1586. Harris Brisbane Dick Fund, 1941. 41.72[3.47])

Launching the *Cleopatra*, which was specially built to carry the London obelisk under tow from Alexandria to England, September 7, 1878. The monument is already inside for the voyage.

by the owner of a bark used to transport granite, the obelisk was to have been lowered directly onto a ship's deck. Aside from the problems of getting the ship close enough to the Alexandrian shore to achieve this goal, and aside from the resulting top-heaviness of the vessel, the deck of the ship in question was simply too small. As Gorringe writes, "It would have been interesting to witness, from the deck of some other vessel, the performances of the bark at sea with the obelisk on her spar-deck."

The second plan required somehow dragging the obelisk into the bay at Alexandria, lifting it with chains until it was suspended beneath the keel of a vessel, and sailing away with the great stone underwater for the voyage. As Gorringe observes somewhat dryly, "no plan was submitted for getting [the obelisk] on the bottom of the bay; and no arrangement was proposed for securing the services of mariners for the voyage." The third proposal involved wrapping the obelisk in enough wood to make it float and then towing it "without steering it."

With his plan approved, Gorringe's first step was to recruit Lieutenant Schroeder, who writes that Gorringe "suddenly appeared in Washington and took me out for a private talk, the subject of which was the removal of the obelisk, and he asked me if I would go with him. That was a call that I could not resist." Nor could Frank Price, who was hired as foreman of ironwork and oversaw the manufacture of the machinery needed to move the obelisk according to Gorringe's designs. The equipment was made by John A. Roebling's Sons and their subcontractors, the Phoenix Iron Works in Trenton, New Jersey. Roebling's was then also in the throes of completing the Brooklyn Bridge.

On October 25, 1836, about 200,000 people squeezed into the Place de la Concorde, Paris, and adjacent streets to witness the raising of Ramesses II's obelisk. The original plan called for using a steam engine, then a new invention and considered, according to a French report, "a mysterious and formidable creation liable to explode like thunder." In fact the engine broke down before it could be tried, and men turning capstans provided the power.

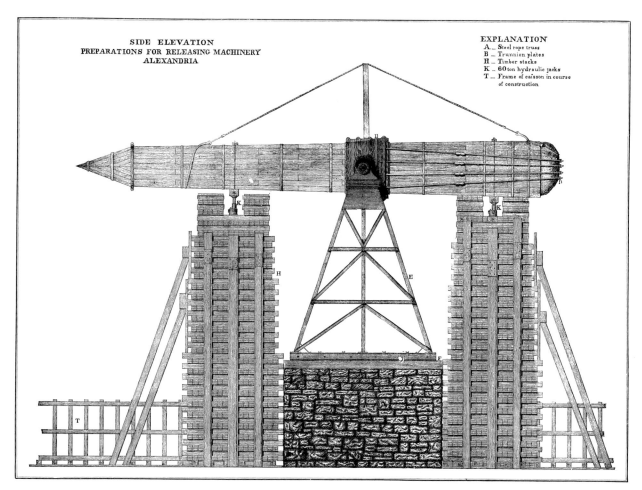

SIDE ELEVATION
PREPARATIONS FOR RELEASING MACHINERY
ALEXANDRIA

EXPLANATION
A — Steel rope truss
B — Trunnion plates
H — Timber stacks
K — 60 ton hydraulic jacks
T — Frame of caisson in course
of construction

After securing leaves of absence from the Navy and with hopes high, Gorringe and Schroeder set sail for England. Although elegant in its simplicity, the plan was still risky. There were also myriad human complications awaiting Gorringe and his team in Alexandria. As one member of a newly formed nationalist group known as the Young Egyptian Party told a reporter from the *New York Herald*, "We Egyptians are just beginning to appreciate our precious monuments and relics and think it a great pity that many of the most valuable ones have already been taken away." The foreign residents, for whatever reason, perhaps simple anti-Americanism, were especially opposed to the obelisk's removal. Despite the khedive's promises, neither they nor the Egyptians were about to let go of Cleopatra's Needle without a struggle.

Gorringe's graceful and efficient turning structure. A pair of trunnions on steel towers (E) were assembled atop masonry foundations (F). Trunnion plates (B) clasped the obelisk at the center of gravity, and four pairs of tie rods on each of two sides of the obelisk connected the trunnion plates to steel heel beams (D) beneath the base. Each tie rod was in two sections that screwed into a turnbuckle where the sections met. Through this system of screws and turnbuckles, the obelisk was raised off its pedestal and rotated on the trunnion pivots into a horizontal position, at which point the turning structure was removed. Hydraulic jacks (K) atop timber (H), stacked up after the obelisk was horizontal, were used to lower the obelisk gradually into a caisson (T).

3. In Pharaoh's Land

*"No one, not even the Khedive, believed
that it would be removed."*

Before departure for Egypt Gorringe and Schroeder searched the docks in vain for an American steamer capable of carrying such a demanding passenger as the obelisk. En route to Alexandria, they stopped in England and continued their search for a ship, going as far as Scotland, but again without success. They crossed the Continent by train to Venice and sailed from there, arriving in Alexandria on October 18, 1879.

"In this interval the Alexandrians had learned that the obelisk was really to be removed," writes Gorringe, "and for the first time in many centuries it became an object of interest.

"The French waited about twenty-five years and the English nearly seventy-five before removing [the] obelisks. . . . There was a feeling in Egypt that the Americans would certainly require a century to perfect their arrangements; and although it was well known that the obelisk had been given to the United States, no one, not even the Khedive, believed that it would be removed.

"Our arrival was the signal for the beginning of an agitation by foreign residents to prevent its removal. Violently abusive articles were published in newspapers, meetings were held, and petitions to the Khedive were circulated for signature; threats of personal violence against any one who attempted to commence the work of re-moval were made openly and by letter, and every other means of frightening us resorted to. . . . On my way to the telegraph office . . . I was greeted with a storm of hisses and a succession of choice epithets [by the younger merchants and brokers]."

Recognizing the urgency of their mission in this hostile climate, Gorringe and Schroeder took the first train to Cairo to see the khedive, Tawfiq Pasha. They returned to Alexandria a day later with a written order commanding the governor of the city to turn the obelisk over to them and to give them the same assistance that had been extended to the English two years earlier. Within three days of their arrival in Egypt, possession of the obelisk had been secured. "As long as it had remained in the control of the Egyptian government there were reasons for anticipating pressure from [Europeans] to prevent its transfer; but the transfer was effected so quickly and so quietly that these gentlemen had no time to act . . . before it was too late. To their protests and petitions subsequently presented, the Khedive and his Ministers answered: 'Too late; Cleopatra's Needle is the possession of the United States officer sent to receive it.'"

No sooner had the American team begun to break ground around the base of the obelisk, however, than they were stopped by a legality. An Italian resident asserted that he owned that particular piece of land. He had actually inherited this claim from a relative who had been given permission earlier in the century to build a bathhouse nearby. When the flimsy structure had washed away in a gale, the man had sought compensation for the sea damage and, when the case remained unresolved, had simply taken possession of the land around Cleopatra's Needle.

Although the case was as unsound as the bathhouse had been, rather than get bogged down in bureaucracy, Gorringe used an age-old remedy. As he wrote to Henry Hurlbert, "If I find the government powerless to oust him I shall try the effect of the greatest of all forces in the East —backsheesh." He "leased" the land from the claimant.

Gorringe and his team were not quite in the clear. As their excavations went forward, a creditor of the Egyptian government demanded possession of the obelisk itself until he was paid. This time, Gorringe took a different tack. He had the United States flag "conspicuously displayed on the obelisk to indicate ownership; and the means of defending it was provided and arranged in a manner that carried conviction to any one that had been in doubt about our sincerity and our determination to defend it and remove it. . . .

"To put an end to these annoyances I determined to push the work of removal forward as rapidly as possible by working night and day, so as to get the obelisk off its pedestal. Every effort was devoted to this end."

Describing the excavations, Gorringe writes, "On the morning of October 29th work was begun by one hundred Arabs, varying from ten to seventy years of age. . . . The middle-aged dug and filled baskets, the old lifted them to the backs of the young, who carried them to the shore and emptied them into the surf. By November 6th an excavation of seventeen hundred and thirty cubic yards had been completed. It had laid bare the pedestal and steps, and made a space large enough to construct a caisson in which to transport the obelisk to the port for embarkation. Several interesting fragments of statuary, a number of coins, and a few scarabee and other antique objects were found by the workmen, to whom liberal rewards were paid for each article delivered. Men accustomed to the work were employed to search the beach for other small objects that having escaped detection would probably be washed up by the surf. In this way many interesting bronze fragments were recovered."

Despite the hard work and the brouhaha, the American team found time for socializing in the cool Egyptian evenings. In his memoirs Schroeder writes about meeting the famous explorer Sir Richard Burton, who "described vividly to me how, in a skirmish with the Somalis, he had had a javelin thrust through his jaw." The German explorer Friedrich Gerhard Rohlfs was

The base, pedestal, and steps uncovered. In 1877 English engineers had filled in the spaces around the base of the standing obelisk with masonry after discovering the loss of two of the bronze sea crabs on which Roman engineers had rested the shaft. Despite the Romans' elaborate measures to keep the crabs in place, determined vandals had managed to pry them loose and replace them with boulders.

The Greek inscription on the outside of the only remaining original claw reads, "In the eighteenth year of [Augustus] Caesar, [P. Rubrius] Barbarus, Prefect of Egypt, erected [it]; Pontius, architect." The inscription is repeated in Latin on the inside surface. Gorringe donated the two original crabs to the Metropolitan Museum, where they have been on almost continuous display since October 1, 1881. (Gift of Commander Henry H. Gorringe, 1881. 81.2.1–2)

exandria on November 11, 1879, just as the pit around the obelisk's pedestal and steps was readied for the next phase in the removal process.

With the exception of the oversize trunnions, the equipment was moved to the work site immediately. A few days later, on a Sunday, when the streets were quiet, the trunnions followed. "The Arabs [doing this work] were very noisy and attracted a large and increasing crowd, who followed the procession through the town. For this an American missionary roundly abused us from a borrowed pulpit, and took advantage of the occasion to denounce the removal of the obelisk as the work of the Devil. This act of 'Christian charity' was of no consequence, beyond the amusement it afforded the editors and readers of local newspapers, who seized on it with much eagerness as evidence of the prevailing sentiment against the Americans. . . . In connection with this question of Sunday-work, which was commented on in a rational manner by many friends, it is well to recall the fact that the Mohammedan and Christian Sabbaths are on different days. It was impossible to observe both; and a respect for the

in Alexandria as well. "He had a notable suavity of manner that colored his every action. While we were chatting one evening in a hotel parlor, a flying bug of some kind alighted on a curtain, and Herr Rohlfs, apparently recognizing a rare specimen, seized it and pinned it to the lapel of his coat with a gentle courtesy that seemed to suggest he was apologizing to the poor thing."

Meanwhile, Frank Price was steaming toward Egypt aboard the *Mariotis*, her hold filled with an assortment of heavy iron parts. To Price, the great towers and trunnions of Gorringe's turning structure resembled "an immense piece of ordnance with the iron towers representing the gun carriage, or [a ship's] old time beam engine with gallows frame." The *Mariotis* docked in Al-

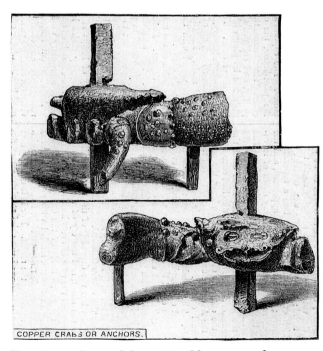

COPPER CRABS OR ANCHORS.

Two views of one of the original bronze crabs.

The obelisk with scaffolding in place. The *New York Herald* (November 1, 1879) reported that "the gallant Commander Gorringe shows himself alive to his duties as an American naval officer. He has hoisted the American flag over the granite column . . . and threatens to shoot on the spot any sacrilegious creditor who proposes to haul [it] down. In other words, the obelisk is now surrounded with a blaze of glory, and Commander Gorringe the central figure in defending the flag. This is an inspiring spectacle."

With Cleopatra's Needle cloaked in protective planking for the journey to America, workmen raise the trunnions into position. The crew hired in Alexandria was generally a conscientious lot, as Frank Price remembered years later, but as soon as they had finished a task they were likely to "move off together to the nearest sand heap and go to sleep regardless of the heat of the tropical sun. A foreman of laborers [and interpreter], known as Said . . . with gorgeous costume suitable for a nobleman, and the manners of a courtier, was often called upon to awaken his men. Selecting a lumber pile, boulder or sand hill to stand on, he addressed his men in Arabic in a very impressive manner, but whether he was advising them to go easy with the work on the principle of 'the more days the more dollars,' or whether he was demanding a greater amount of energy was never known and as the result was the same it made but little difference."

The obelisk beginning to pivot.

to pull the upper end over by means of tackles. This attempt failed, owing to the . . . bending of the heel-beams, which caused the bottom of the obelisk to bind against the top of one of the crabs. The impression prevailed that the turning structure had settled and was therefore of inadequate strength to sustain the weight. Several engineers and others strongly advised abandoning the attempt to place the obelisk horizontal in the manner proposed; and letters were received protesting against the destruction of so valuable a monument by any further attempt to remove it. These expressions did not affect in any way the confidence I felt in a speedy termination of this, the first stage of the work, although they caused me great chagrin, and aroused every one associated with me in the work to an extra exertion in order to prove them senseless."

Once the crabs were removed the obelisk moved easily. A stack of timbers was placed to cushion the obelisk's fall in the event of a mishap, and all was almost ready for the stone's first true shift in position in almost two thousand years. It only remained to safeguard the work area. During the years of survey work in the Mediterranean Gorringe had made many friends in other fleets, and one of these friendships now proved most reassuring. "Rumors of a possible demonstration by the foreign residents when the obelisk was to be placed horizontal had been circulated until they reached Rear-Admiral Aslambekoff, of the Russian Imperial Navy, who was in the port of Alexandria in his flag-ship the 'Minim.' He was aware of the feeling that existed among the foreigners, and while unable to land an armed force for our protection, he landed a large force of unarmed trained seamen for the purpose of enclosing the grounds in a cordon of effective men and affording any assistance that was needed at a critical moment."

On the morning of December 6, moments after the arrival of the governor of Alexandria, "the word was given to slack the tackles. A large crowd of Greeks, Italians, and other Europeans had gathered in the vicinity, and occupied every

opinions of both sects led to the rule that work would be carried on without intermission, and that the workmen were at liberty to select their own Sunday and observe it in their own fashion. Arab Mohammedans and Maltese and European Christians formed the majority of the men employed. The former spent Friday, their Sabbath, in a rational manner, sleeping during the early part of the day, attending services at the mosque at noon, and devoting the afternoon to social intercourse and amusement. The Christians, almost to a man, would devote the thirty-six hours from Saturday evening to Monday morning in drinking, gambling, fighting, and other excesses, and return to work drunk, sleepy, and bruised."

By December 2 the turning structure had been assembled atop newly laid masonry foundations. Two days later, with the obelisk raised from its pedestal and readied, "an attempt was made available spot from which the movement could be seen. While we were waiting for the Governor, the crowd was noisy and at times unruly. . . . But at the instant the obelisk began to move there was absolute silence and stillness. As it slowly turned not a sound but the rendering of the ropes around the posts and an occasional creak of the structure could be heard. Immediately following a creak louder than any previous one, the motion was suddenly arrested, then there was a sharp snap—one of the tackles had parted. Instantly the order was given to slack the other tackle rapidly, using it merely to retard the motion and not to arrest it; but the man attending the fall had lost his wits, and instead of slackening, he held it fast and it very soon broke. The obelisk was at that moment about half over; it moved slowly at first and then more and more rapidly, until it struck the stack of timbers, rebounded twice, and came to rest. . . . There was intense excitement; many of the [crowd] had fled precipitously when the obelisk began to move rapidly; and when it [came to rest] . . . there arose a prolonged cheer, which was the first friendly manifestation shown by the Alexandrians.

"The explanation given for the breaking of the first tackle by the man attending it was, that he looked up to see what the noise was, and in

With the obelisk horizontal, the flag was hoisted again. The tie rods and heel beams are clearly visible. The apartment building under construction stands in the lot that was once home to the London obelisk.

Another view of the obelisk resting on the strategically placed stack of timber that broke its fall when the tackles gave way.

doing so involuntarily checked the passage of the rope through his hands; this brought the whole strain on his tackle and caused it to break. The other man was properly giving his whole attention to the command, and was unconscious of the accident until he saw that his companion had fled precipitately from under the obelisk, leaving him alone. Surely his loss of self-control was excusable."

The stack of timber had done its work and the stone had pivoted smoothly, without injury to itself or to any of the work crew or spectators.

The obelisk was now horizontal but it still hovered some forty-three feet overhead. To lower it, hydraulic pumps atop two newly raised, tapering towers of timber were used. Once the obelisk was resting on the timber, the trunnions and turning structure were dismantled and packed away. The pumps then raised the obelisk, timber was removed nine inches at a time, and the pumps lowered the stone again to rest on the timber stack. The pumps themselves were then lowered and the process repeated.

Each stage of the removal process had been plagued with obstacles, from the spurious claims of ownership to inadequate supplies and insufficient cooperation. The lowering process, for example, was especially slow because Gorringe had been denied the sturdy timber used by the English in 1877 in removing the fallen obelisk. Wood being a rare commodity in Egypt at any time, this stash had been carefully kept in storage until the khedive ordered it turned over to Gorringe. However, "the officer in charge happened to be a European, and he managed to evade the order. . . by delays and other means, until it was too late. . . . The only [other timber] available was the soft planks that were bought at an exorbitant rate."

Europeans were responsible for an even more costly delay. The foreign merchants who kept the city's streets paved and clean also controlled their use. They refused to give Gorringe a permit to move the obelisk over the streets, claiming its weight would damage the water mains, and no amount of persuasion could budge them. Gorringe was forced to find another way to transport the obelisk to the harbor side of the city.

His solution was to build a caisson to receive the obelisk as it was lowered and float it around the bay. While the obelisk moved downward in stately fashion at the rate of three feet a day, the masonry foundation that had anchored the turning structure was demolished, the excavation pit was enlarged, and work was begun on the caisson. The pedestal, freed of its burden of almost two thousand years, was rolled on cannonballs to one side of the pit. Beneath it was found an interesting arrangement of marked stones and a trowel that some thought related to the ancient origins of Freemasonry. Struck with the symbolism, Gorringe decided to take the pedestal, steps, and foundation to the New World and reposition them as they had been. No other obelisk has traveled with its original foundation and been raised in such a manner.

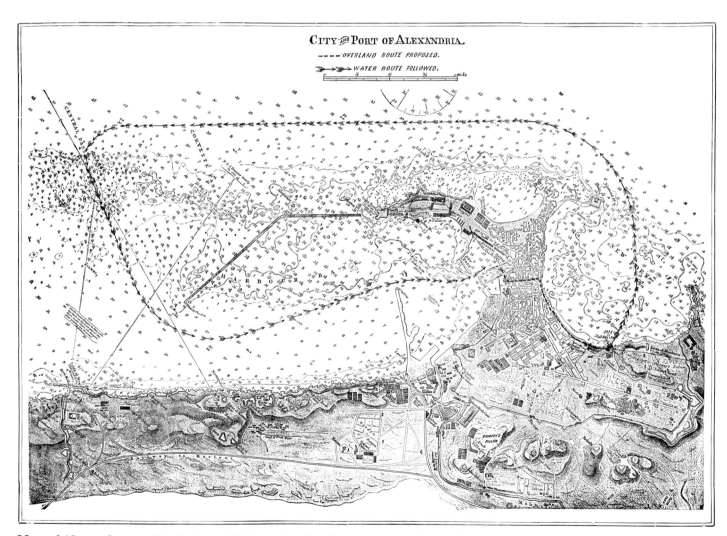

Map of Alexandria and its harbor, 1879, marked by Gorringe to indicate the proposed overland route and the water route that required clearing a passage through submerged ruins. "The foundation of one very large building is distinctly traceable underwater when the sea is smooth," writes Gorringe, "and about 100 yards from the beach there is a broken column sticking up from the bottom of the sea, nearly equal in diameter to Pompey's pillar."

A street in the heart of Alexandria around the turn of the century. Even though "the distance overland was less than a mile, and the route was over comparatively unfrequented streets, except for a short distance across what was once the ancient causeway," Gorringe was denied permission to transport the obelisk by land.

4. Departure

"A boat load of the Arabs who had been employed on the work all the time we were in Alexandria accompanied us to the entrance of the port, and hastily took their departure when the vessel began to feel the swell and to roll."

The new approach to the obelisk's embarkation meant maneuvering the caisson across a bay that was littered with submerged Roman ruins. Gorringe hired divers and equipment to move chunks of old temples and other buildings and to grade the launchway. "The diving operations . . . were carried on continuously when the state of the sea would permit; but it was a common occurrence for one day of heavy surf to destroy the results of many days' work. Nothing more disheartening can be imagined than to witness the destruction in a few hours of the results of many days of costly labor without the possibility of preventing it." By mid-March, however, Cleopatra's Needle was in its caisson and ready to launch.

A ramp had been built and slathered with grease to allow the caisson to slip easily into the bay. "I regard this part of the work," writes Gorringe, "that is, the operation of placing the caisson on the launching ways and launching it, as attended with more . . . risks than any other. We were restricted to an inadequate space for carrying on the work conveniently; we were operating on an exposed coast in the stormiest season

(March), with the sea breaking dangerously at least two thirds of the time; and we were without sufficient hydraulic power to lower the sea end of the caisson without great risk."

On the morning of March 18, the caisson was untied and "under pressure from [the pumps, it] began to move very slowly at first, then more rapidly, and after it had slid a distance of twenty feet it abruptly stopped sliding. . . . At this critical time the sea, which had been smooth, began to rise rapidly, and the tug [waiting to tow the caisson] was obliged to seek shelter in Alexandria's harbor. By dark the sea had become so rough that all efforts to get the caisson afloat had to be suspended. By the next morning the sea had moderated, and our efforts to push the caisson into the water were renewed, in the belief that it would slide of its own accord if it could be started with rapid motion. But in this we were mistaken."

As they later learned, the ramp had been stripped and befouled by debris washing up with the surf. Over the next thirteen days the caisson had to be inched laboriously down the launchway. Raging winter seas and bad weather, especially a gale the night of March 21, caused work stoppages and great anxiety for the safety of the obelisk and crew. At times the caisson thumped ominously against the launchway, but on the morning of March 31, it finally let go its grip of the shore and floated free. By afternoon it had been towed the ten miles to Alexandria's port and was safely moored, at least for the moment.

"While the operations of lowering the obelisk and launching the caisson had been progressing, preparations were being made for embarking the obelisk on the steamer 'Dessoug.' This vessel had been purchased from the Egyptian government expressly for transporting the obelisk to New York. She is an iron steamer built in England in 1864 for the Egyptian government, and had been employed chiefly in the Egyptian postal service between Alexandria, Smyrna, and Constantinople. Extravagance and corruption in the service had caused the withdrawal of several of the steamers employed in it, the 'Dessoug' among them."

Gorringe and Schroeder, who had renewed their efforts to find a suitable ship as soon as they arrived in Alexandria, had first seen the *Dessoug* "lying dismantled in the arsenal," the port's navy yard. By their calculations, her dimensions suited their purposes, although "her engines and boilers were known to be in bad condition . . . her hold was filthy, and she had been neglected to a degree that cannot be imagined."

There had been a plan afoot by a group of ship brokers to prevent Gorringe from purchasing the *Dessoug*, or at least to force him to pay an extraordinarily high price for it, but he proved once again to be a skillful and daring negotiator. To avoid protests, "the conclusion of the purchase and time fixed for transfer were kept secret. The transfer was effected in the office of the Director of the Postal Service, whose representative accompanied me on board, and hauled down the Egyptian flag, while I hoisted United States ensigns to the mast-heads and peaks. The Arabs in immediate charge of the vessel looked on in amazement at this performance. When ordered to gather up their personal effects and leave the vessel, they made no protest, but deferred their departure until they had prayed fervently and impressively. . . . A notice in Arabic, Greek, Italian, French, and English was posted on each gang-

Lowering the pedestal into the hold of the Dessoug.

GIRDERS SUPPORTING PEDESTAL.

FORWARD BETWEEN DECKS—THE FOUNDATION STONES.

The pedestal was secured in an iron frame for the voyage, and the stones of the steps and foundation were evenly distributed to bring "the vessel to a good trim."

way, prohibiting any one from going on board without a pass from Lieutenant Schroeder, at the peril of their lives."

Getting the ship registered was "a delicate question to settle. Under the laws of the United States she could not be registered as an American vessel. Sailing under the Egyptian flag would have involved serious risks. . . . The British or other European flag would have been more objectionable from every standpoint. . . . There was no other course than open defiance of law . . . and I determined to make the voyage from Alexandria to New York without registry or nationality."

With the *Dessoug* repaired and refitted to take on its ancient passenger, it was ready to move into dry dock in Alexandria, but stalling tactics by officials of the port caused further delays. The *Dessoug* had to stand by while several small steamers had their hulls cleaned, a job that could as easily have been done on the shore as in the dry dock. The wait would be five weeks.

During this time Gorringe persuaded the official in charge to allow him to move just the caisson into dry dock. It was "leaking badly and there was danger of its being sunk by accident or design as long as it was afloat. As soon as it was in the dock it was demolished, not so much to advance the work of embarkation as to insure the

obelisk not being removed from the dock until it had been embarked in the 'Dessoug.'"

Gorringe then set about moving the pedestal and steps to the harbor. He hired a lighter, or barge, which was hauled up the same ramp that had been used to launch the caisson. With the hydraulic pumps, the pedestal was raised and loaded onto the lighter. Once the steps and other stones in the foundation, along with the dismantled turning structure, were loaded, the lighter was towed to the harbor.

The transfer of the pedestal to the *Dessoug* while she waited her turn in the dry dock was somewhat trickier to accomplish. The pedestal alone weighed nearly fifty tons, and no single crane in Alexandria was capable of hoisting it. With customary aplomb, Gorringe combined the efforts of a crane on the dock and a floating steam-derrick crane that together could lift fifty-five tons. In the first attempt, the pedestal was tied with cable and lifted clear of the barge.

As the barge made way for the stern of the *Dessoug*, "a sharp sound was heard and the pedestal was observed to be oscillating. It was known positively that nothing had touched it to cause oscillation or vibration. If it had fallen while the steamer's stern was under it the destruction of that end of the vessel would have been the result.

Sliding the obelisk on cannonballs into the hold of the *Dessoug*.

The 'Dessoug' was hauled ahead as rapidly as possible; when her stern was well clear and nothing remained between the pedestal and the water, an examination was made, and one of the four parts of the steel-wire rope . . . was found to have stranded. Only two of the seven strands remained uninjured. The pedestal was then lowered in the full expectation that it would fall into the water. . . . But the two strands held on." It was placed back on the barge and the next day, using the *Dessoug*'s heaviest anchor chain, it was safely transferred into the hold.

Once the *Dessoug* entered dry dock and "was high and dry the work [of making an opening in the starboard hull] began, and was carried on without intermission day and night . . . until the aperture had been opened. About seven thousand rivets, sixteen frames, and thirty plates had to be removed. . . .

"The space that intervened between the obelisk and the aperture was bridged over with heavy timbers. . . . The bed of the track was thus a continuous one from where the obelisk had been landed on the dock, through the aperture, and into the hold. As soon as this track had been completed, the obelisk was raised by the hydraulic pumps, and while suspended on them the channel irons and cannon-balls . . . were placed under it on each side, near the edges."

With everything in position, it took a mere eight hours to slide the obelisk into the hull through the opening. The starboard hull was riveted closed and within days the *Dessoug* was afloat again.

Finding a crew had proved to be one of the most difficult challenges, "the cause of endless trouble and negotiation from the day the vessel was purchased until the day she sailed. . . . The chief engineer, a Scotchman, had been in the Egyptian postal service, and had served several years on the 'Dessoug' while she was employed in that service. . . . The first and second officers, the second and third engineers, and three quartermasters [came from] England. The first and second officers turned out to be confirmed drunkards; the latter so bad that he had to be dismissed to prevent him from killing himself. He fell twice from the second deck into the hold, and twice overboard while drunk. The engineers were useful, hard-working, hard-drinking men. The quartermasters would do credit to a pirate's crew. The number of men who solemnly enlisted for the voyage and speedily deserted before it began, was forty-eight. Despairing of being able to secure a crew in Alexandria, I sent my power of attorney to Trieste. . . . I relied on having these men arrive upon the day the vessel was ready for sea, and on getting away from the port before they had time to think about it. They arrived, however, the day the vessel was floated out of the dock. All but three remained. . . . As the 'Dessoug' had no nationality, deserters could not be arrested. [Only] four of the crew, besides the quartermasters, could speak or understand a word of English. It must be evident that, considering the circumstances,

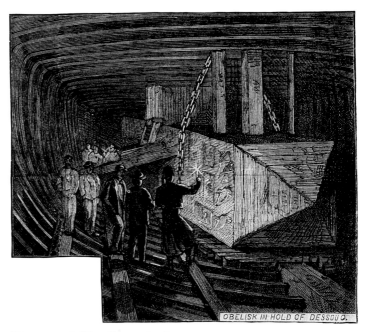

OBELISK IN HOLD OF DESSOUG.

Cleopatra's Needle made the ocean crossing in style, on a "bed of Adriatic white pine, very spongy and soft. . . . To prevent it from moving laterally, a system of horizontal, diagonal, and vertical shores were fitted into the hieroglyphs and driven against the stringer pieces of the steamer's hull." It was a snug fit, leaving room for little else.

commanding the 'Dessoug' was not the most desirable and comfortable of occupations."

Gorringe had almost as much difficulty with the insurance agents, who were unwilling to insure the *Dessoug* unless paid an exorbitant rate. After trying to negotiate reasonably, Gorringe simply set his own price and threatened to sail without insurance "on the next day." This brought him "a great many acceptances of two per cent., and insurance was effected by telegraph at this rate in a number of selected companies. Finally, at 2 P.M., of Saturday, June 12th, the moorings were cast off and the 'Dessoug' steamed out of port amidst the sounding of steam-whistles, the cheers of ships' crews and boatmen, and a general dipping of colors. . . . A boat load of the Arabs who had been employed on the work all the time we were in Alexandria accompanied us to the entrance of the port, and hastily took their departure when the vessel began to feel the swell and to roll. To Lieutenant Schroeder and myself the open sea, with the comparative rest and relief that it brought, was acceptable and enjoyable beyond expression."

5. At Sea

" . . . she was held to her course and driven through the gale as hard as the boilers would permit."

After 241 days in Egypt Gorringe, Schroeder, and their rare cargo were finally heading for New York. Writes Gorringe, "The wind freshened and the sea increased gradually as we drew away from the land. The behavior of the vessel was most satisfactory; her pitching motion was slow and easy, her rolling exceptionally gentle. Perfect confidence in the efficiency of the stowage and the ability of the steamer to make the voyage with no greater risk than is involved in any similar voyage, was quickly acquired by the crew, who settled down to the monotonous routine of an ordinary merchant-steamer."

Ten days later, having successfully sailed through a Mediterranean gale and a night of violent thunderstorms and squalls, they dropped anchor off Gibraltar where they had arranged to take on coal. "The only unpleasant feature of this passage was the leaking of both boilers in every furnace, which prevented them from making adequate steam. There was no excuse for this condition of the boilers. The chief engineer had been allowed all the labor and material he wanted to put them in efficient condition, had expended enough to do so, and had reported them thoroughly repaired."

It took three extra days to make the necessary repairs, and during this time, "a large number of people visited the ship to see the obelisk, among them Lord Napier of Magdala, the Governor, and his staff, accompanied by Lady Napier and a number of other ladies.

"We sailed from Gibraltar at midnight of June 25–26th. . . . On June 30th we passed through the Azores, the weather having been variable and at times disagreeable. On July 6th, at 8.30 P.M., when 1,500 miles from New York, with a smooth sea and a moderately fair wind, the engines came to an abrupt standstill after a short interval of unusual and noisy performance. Examination showed that the after-crank shaft had broken through an old flaw or crack. . . . Fortunately, the breaking of the shaft was the only damage done, and there were two spare sections of shaft on board, one of which belonged to the after engine."

For almost a week the *Dessoug* more or less drifted, auxiliary sails aloft. Another ship was encountered, and Schroeder went aboard with a telegram for the captain to send as soon as he reached his first port, giving the position of the

Visitors boarding the *Dessoug* to see the obelisk.

Dessoug. The bond among mariners is strong, and as Schroeder later recalled, "while chatting with the Captain, I mentioned that if he had any bread to spare we would be glad to buy some. He ordered some bags brought up and put in my boat; but when I offered to settle for it he replied that, as he had plenty, he could not think of taking pay for bread from a ship in distress."

With the *Dessoug* still powerless, a patch of squally weather caused Gorringe "more anxiety than any thing else during the voyage, much more than the breaking of the shaft. . . . Water-spouts were seen to form and dissipate without completing the column several times during the day. One formed directly to windward of the vessel, and after appearing to dissipate, it suddenly reformed much larger than before, and began moving directly toward us. . . . After watching it closely it was evident that we were in for a deluge unless the course of the vessel could be changed. This was impossible owing to the lack of wind, which had in the meantime entirely died out. There was nothing to do but to await the deluge calmly, for we had no cannon to fire and break the spout. It kept us in suspense for about five minutes, and then abruptly changed its course, passed about fifty yards ahead of us, and broke with some noise about a thousand yards from the vessel. The danger feared was in the probable bursting in of our decks by the weight of the column of water which appeared at least fifty feet in height."

On July 12, the repairs were completed and the *Dessoug* started ahead again under steam, pushing into a westerly gale for the next three days. "The behavior of the vessel was exceptionally good, as far as her motion was concerned," writes Gorringe, "but [two large waves broke on her decks], which did considerable damage to boats and skylights. Very close watch was kept of the obelisk and its fastenings, but not the least motion was detected in any thing connected with them. With the fullest confidence that the vessel was able to stand any weather, she was held to her course and driven through the gale as hard as the boilers would permit, so as to reach port on

The broken crank shaft.

the day set for our arrival—not later than July 20th—and to avoid the usual but needless anxieties experienced by landsmen when vessels are overdue."

His arrival timed to perfection, Gorringe picked up a New York harbor pilot on the morning of July 19, and that evening while passing Fire Island, the ship made a prearranged signal announcing her imminent arrival in the city. By 2:00 A.M. on July 20 she was anchored off Staten Island.

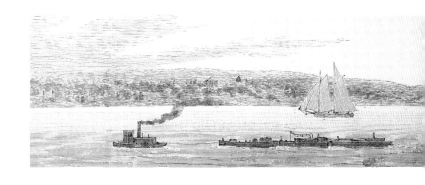

The erratic behavior of the *Cleopatra* at sea contrasts dramatically with the serene voyage of the *Dessoug*. During a gale in the Bay of Biscay the English vessel had to be abandoned, but after drifting for several days, it was recovered by a passing steamer and towed to London unharmed. The French had also had horrendous problems with their custom-made vessel, the *Luxor*. According to Gorringe, it was "reported to have rolled so violently that her crew had difficulty holding on."

The *Dessoug* leaving Alexandria. "We were a happy quartet upon putting to sea from Alexandria on June 12, 1880," writes Seaton Schroeder, "Gorringe, myself, Mr. Price and Mr. Davis, foremen respectively of iron work and wood work."

6. Time Capsules

" . . . a small box, the contents of which [are] known only to himself."

Walt Whitman called New York a "city of wharves and stores . . . A proud and passionate city—mettlesome, mad, extravagant city." In 1880 it was among the busiest seaports on the East Coast. Lower Manhattan rose behind a bristling hedge of ships' masts. The Brooklyn Bridge was nearing completion, and on Bedloe's Island in the bay, a great statue would soon lift a welcoming lamp to incoming ships.

Far uptown, in the area around Central Park, was a different city, an odd patchwork of vacant lots, new apartment buildings, stately mansions, parkland, farms, and shantytowns. At Eighty-second Street and Fifth Avenue, The Metropolitan Museum of Art opened the doors to its new home on March 30, 1880, its trustees half wondering whether anyone would travel to what was then considered "too suburban a location" to see its collections.

The Museum's trustees need not have worried. The Museum was soon to have a new neighbor with a commanding presence that would attract crowds of visitors. Cleopatra's Needle was to be raised in Central Park, on Graywacke Knoll, one of the highest spots in Manhattan. Although graywacke is a kind of sandstone, the knoll is actually an outcrop of the granite for which Manhattan

is famous. This location would keep the obelisk isolated from the city's rapidly rising architecture—it would never be dwarfed by skyscrapers.

The site, west of the Museum, had been chosen quietly in 1879, winning out over such candidates as Columbus Circle, Grand Army Plaza, and Union Square. An indoor location may also have been considered as early as 1879; at least this is suggested by a letter from Hurlbert to General Louis Palma di Cesnola, the Metropolitan Museum's director: "It would be mischief to put such a monument under a roof and it is not to be thought of," wrote Hurlbert, adding, with a touch of hyperbole, "The talk about the atmosphere is chiefly all nonsense. The obelisk . . . has been snowed on, rained on, blown on, and blazed on ever since Constantine the Meek without doing it any essential harm." Within two years of the obelisk's installation, he would be proven wrong.

With the site chosen, it remained only to bring Cleopatra's Needle to its new home. The *Dessoug*, meanwhile, moored off Twenty-third Street on the Hudson River, attracted a steady stream of visitors who descended into the dark hold to marvel at the obelisk. At the end of July, the ship moved to a wharf at the end of Fifty-first Street to discharge the first of its colossal passengers—the pedestal, steps, and foundation. A derrick had been borrowed from the city, and as Gorringe writes, "the pedestal was lifted out of the steamer and landed on the dock by the derrick with an ease and rapidity that contrasted strangely with its embarkation in Alexandria."

From the wharf the pedestal "was moved by sliding it on heavy timbers (skids) to a convenient place about five hundred feet distant, there to await the partial rebuilding of a truck that was to carry it to the Central Park. This truck was the only one in the city capable of sustaining a load of fifty tons that was suitable for moving the pedestal. . . . Difficulty was experienced in several places in keeping the wheels from sinking into the pavements. They had only to sink nine inches for the chain slings, by which the stone

TOP OF THE PEDESTAL.

SCENE ON DECK.

SIDE VIEW OF THE PEDESTAL.

STEAMSHIP DESSOUG.

was suspended to the beams, to touch the ground. Whenever this occurred the slings had to be slackened until the truck was released, and the wheels placed on timber laid on the pavement, and the stone again suspended. . . . The route was through Fifty-first Street to Fifth Avenue, through Fifth Avenue to the Eighty-second Street east entrance to the park, where the truck was dispensed with. Thence to the site the pedestal was moved on greased skids."

From the moment of the *Dessoug*'s arrival in New York, Cleopatra's Needle was the best show in town. Everyone longed to catch a glimpse of it. Even the *Dessoug* seemed exotic. A writer for the *New York Herald* (July 21, 1879) called her "a black and ponderous craft that used to carry Egyptian troops and mail twixt Oriental ports. . . . Though it is easy to discern her English pattern, somehow her Eastern voyages have partly worn away her European birthmarks. . . . The Staten Island ferryboat *Northfield* was first to greet her, and hundreds of passengers waved their hats and handkerchiefs in passing, and scrutinized her heavy sides as if they could peer through upon her precious treasure."

ARRIVAL OF THE DESSOUG WITH THE OBELISK ON BOARD

THE OBELISK ON BOARD THE DESSOUG

Graywacke Knoll had been prepared by removing the topsoil and leveling the exposed granite. Cracks and cavities were filled with cement, which was also spread in a thin layer on the surface. Then, "the foundation was replaced exactly as it had stood in Alexandria, each piece in the same relative position to the others, and to the points of the compass. . . . Each piece was bound to the other by iron and steel clamps similar to those that had been used by the Romans, which we had necessarily removed when taking the foundation apart in Alexandria.

"A number of lead boxes of different shapes and sizes had been prepared to fit into available spaces enclosed by the steps, and into these were placed the various articles contributed by the Departments in Washington and by individuals. . . . Applications for space in them came from all over the country. Some were evidently prompted by vanity, others by a hope of advertisement, but the majority were based on a common-sense desire to perpetuate some examples of our civilization."

These time capsules contain an odd assortment of memorabilia: a proof set of U.S. coins for 1880, a facsimile of the Declaration of Independence, letters from the khedive, a selection of medals from the different branches of the armed services, a compendium of the 1870 census, various weather maps, a model of the propeller from Admiral Farragut's flagship, documents from the A.S.P.C.A., Freemason's emblems, industrial metal samples, a selection of screws and other hardware, a hydraulic pump, a set of Bierstadt's photographs of the project, and a flurry of papers and documents from various agencies. Books used as filler included the Bible, Webster's dictionary, Shakespeare's complete works, an encyclopedia of mechanics and engineering, and a guide to Egypt. Finally, William Henry Hurlbert contributed a mysterious "small box, the contents of which [are] known only to himself."

The Freemasons had a strong presence in New York in 1880. Almost to a man, all those involved in bringing Cleopatra's Needle to America were members—Gorringe, Schroeder, Vanderbilt,

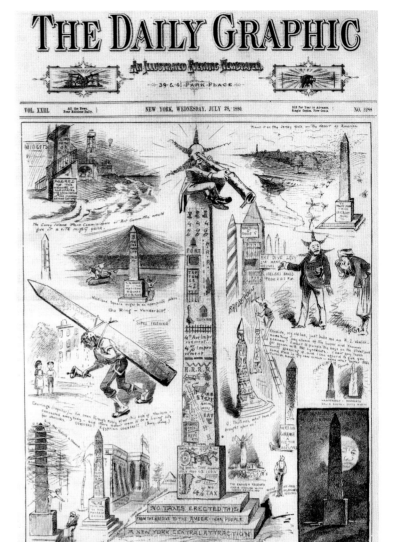

Although a site in Central Park had been decided upon long before the obelisk's arrival, the selection process was replayed by a cartoonist for *The Daily Graphic* (July 28, 1880).

Opposite: When a reporter for the *New York World* (July 22, 1880) visited the *Dessoug*, he wrote, "With lighted candles as cautiously carried as though the ship's cargo were gunpowder instead of corrugated stone, one or the other of the watchmen politely showed each visitor down into the dark region in which the obelisk lies. . . . The visitors for the most part did not have the appearance of being Egyptologists but they were invariably curious to get a glimpse of the great stone and they invariably returned to the dock in a wild state of enthusiasm."

Above: Moving the pedestal on skids from the wharf. Gorringe claimed that the "stone is the largest and heaviest moved on wheels of which there is any record, and excepting the obelisk it is the largest ever moved through New York City."

Opposite (top): Transporting the pedestal required "thirty-two horses in sixteen pairs. . . . The first forward movement was invariably given by hydraulic pumps applied to the tire of the rear wheels. As soon as the truck was in motion the horses were started and kept going on a slow trot until the wheels again sank into the pavements."

Opposite (bottom): Preparing to lower the cornerstone, October 10, 1880. For the Freemasons the cube of polished marble that had been found under the pedestal was thought to represent one of their most significant symbols, the Perfect Ashlar.

and Hurlbert, as well as the mayor, commissioner of police, and others in city politics. The Masons' interest in the obelisk had been intensified by the trowel, markings, and arrangement of stones beneath the pedestal. It is not surprising that the local members were invited to lay the foundation for the obelisk.

On October 9, 1880, a parade of nine thousand Freemasons marched up Fifth Avenue, bands blaring, to Graywacke Knoll for a grand and solemn cornerstone ceremony. On October 11 the pedestal was swung into position and by the end of the month the turning structure, brought from Alexandria, had been reassembled to await the arrival of the obelisk of Thutmosis III, nearing the end of its long journey from the Aswan quarries.

THE PROCESSION PASSING THE METROPOLITAN MUSEUM.

The foundation-laying ceremony. The grand marshal linked the origins of Freemasonry to ancient Egypt.

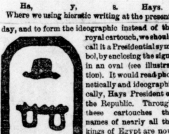

Ha, y, s. Hays.
Where we using hieratic writing at the present day, and to form the ideographic instead of the royal cartouch, we should call it a Presidential symbol, by enclosing the signs in an oval (see illustration). It would read phonetically and ideographically, Hays President of the Republic. Through these cartouches the names of nearly all the kings of Egypt are now known, many who lived long before the time of Moses. Skeptics averred, when the discovery of hieroglyphical reading was made, that it would disprove the truth of the Scriptures. On the contrary, some of the first elucidations went strongly to corroborate the sacred history, and many synchronisms have been proved thereby.

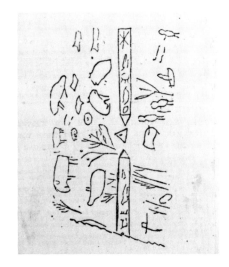

With the arrival of the obelisk, the *Evening Post* (November 3, 1880) applied hieroglyphs to contemporary themes. The president's name might be misspelled in the text, but the cartouche is impeccable. Not long afterward, President Rutherford B. Hayes commented on the safe arrival of Cleopatra's Needle in his final "Message to Congress" delivered December 6, 1880.

The hieroglyphs on Cleopatra's Needle inspired all manner of fanciful translations. One "expert" in *The Daily Graphic* (August 28, 1880) claimed that the New York obelisk describes the wanderings of ancient Mexicans from Central America to Alaska and across Asia to Egypt, which was identified as "an outgrowth of Mexico." The claim was "supported" by a stone supposedly found buried on a farm in Davenport, Iowa, on which two obelisks appear and by a drawing of an inscription alleged to have been seen in Alaska.

In the *Mercury* (August 15, 1880), under the headline, "The Obelisk Speaks," two other "experts" claimed that the hieroglyphs on Cleopatra's Needle foretold the future of America. In reality, they are more like ancient publicity blurbs for the pharaoh. The east face, for example, boasts that "he is the heavenly Horus, the powerful and glorious bull. He is the king of Upper and Lower Egypt . . . the Sun himself, and the child of the gods" and so forth. Charles Moldenke, whose 1891 book on the New York obelisk was one of the earliest, writes "It is just this . . . barefaced king-worship represented by the obelisk that gives its translation such a repulsive sound to modern ears. No wonder that otherwise well-read and intelligent men turn about in amazement and ask: 'Can this really be the correct translation of the obelisks?'"

It was almost inevitable that thread manufacturers would use images of Cleopatra's Needle as a promotional ploy. A series of trade cards from different manufacturers retells the story of the obelisk's journey from Egypt to Central Park, where a spool of thread walks a bulldog near the newly raised needle. (The Jefferson R. Burdick Collection, Gift of Jefferson R. Burdick)

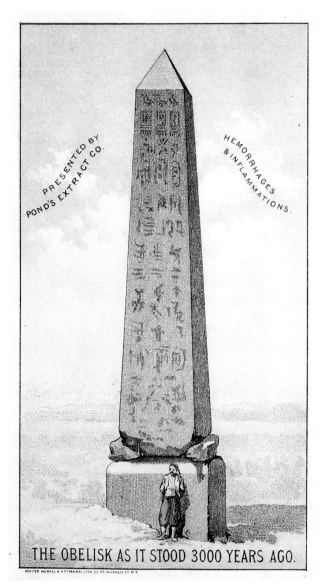

THE OBELISK AS IT STOOD 3000 YEARS AGO.

Patent medicine companies, such as Pond's Extract, also used pictures of the obelisk to sell their products.

A folding model of Cleopatra's Needle dating to the time of the obelisk's arrival.

7. Landfall and Transport

"I determined to make the rising tide lift the obelisk and the falling tide land it."

There was only one place in Manhattan to beach the obelisk. The dramatic tides of the East River eliminated the most convenient landing places, and although the banks of the Hudson River were treacherously steep, there was one break: at Ninety-sixth Street. It was here that Gorringe proposed landing his cargo, after first transferring it from the *Dessoug* to a barge.

There was a new problem, however, reminiscent of those encountered in Alexandria. The owner of the only suitable dry dock in the city, an opportunist, had raised his rates and demanded a security against damages. "At first I thought of taking the 'Dessoug' to Philadelphia or Baltimore," writes Gorringe, "disembarking the obelisk in the spacious dry dock in either of these cities, and bringing it to New York on floats by canal. Negotiations with the dock owners [there] developed the same feeling as those existing in New York as to extra charges."

After rejecting various alternatives, Gorringe devised a most elegant solution to the problem, one that harnessed the forces of nature and required only a marine railway, consisting of a track,

engine, and winch, and used to haul ships from the sea for cleaning and repairs. "Disembarking the obelisk while the 'Dessoug' was on a marine railway was entirely practicable and as easily accomplished as if the steamer were in a dock. But getting the obelisk afloat with moderate expense after it had been disembarked, so as to remove it to the foot of Ninety-sixth Street, was the difficult problem to solve. After having almost despaired of being able to accomplish my object without yielding to the demands of the dock company, I reached a solution that may be summed up in the word *tide*. I determined to make the rising tide lift the obelisk and the falling tide land it. There would be no lack of power."

Gorringe leased a marine railway on Staten Island and on August 22 the first rivet was removed from the *Dessoug*'s starboard side. Two weeks later Cleopatra's Needle emerged from the hold and was rolled on cannonballs onto heavy cross timbers positioned atop pilings. Two long pontoons were positioned between the pilings and filled with water.

On September 16, "every thing being ready and the weather favorable, the pontoons were pumped out at low-water and adjusted to their proper position under the obelisk. The rising tide caused them gradually to raise the cross-timbers clear of the capping on the piles until the weight of the obelisk had been transferred from the stage [to the pontoons]. At high-water, 4 P.M., they were hauled out of the slip into the bay, bearing the obelisk on their decks. . . .

"A landing-stage had been prepared for the obelisk at the foot of Ninety-sixth Street . . . identically the same in principle as that at Staten Island. . . .

"The time of high-water [there] is about two hours later than at Staten Island. The distance is twelve miles. At 4.55 P.M. the [steamer] 'Manhattan' started ahead with the pontoons in tow. We reached the landing-stage at Ninety-sixth Street at 7.15 P.M.. The evening was very dark and it seemed as if it would be impossible to adjust the pontoons between the rows of piles. After one or

The *Dessoug* being hauled up a marine railway on Staten Island to begin the final phase of the project.

two failures, owing to the swiftly running tide, this was finally accomplished. . . . The valves of the pontoons were opened to admit water to them and in a few minutes the obelisk had been finally landed on Manhattan Island. As it settled down on the staging the piles swayed, owing to their great height; but as soon as the whole weight was on them they remained steady and the staging became stable.

"The Hudson River Railway tracks skirt the river bank at the point where the obelisk was landed; passenger trains pass at very frequent intervals, the longest time between trains being an hour and a half about noon. To have blocked the road at this point for more than two or three hours would have involved serious loss and much serious inconvenience to travellers."

Gorringe devised a bridge that could be thrown across the railroad line as soon as train traffic was halted. The next day the obelisk was again rolled on cannonballs in channels from the staging on the riverbank, across the tracks, to the roadway of Ninety-sixth Street. The entire procedure took one hour and twenty minutes, delaying a single freight train a mere twenty-five minutes.

The short trip over the tracks had revealed a flaw in the method. The great weight of the obelisk repeatedly split the channels in which the cannonballs rolled. No amount of reinforcement

Cleopatra's Needle emerges before a large welcoming committee. "The report that the obelisk was to be disembarked," writes Gorringe, "brought down to Staten Island a crowd of spectators, who occupied every available spot from which a view of the work could be obtained." At this point cannonballs were still part of the plans for moving it.

Cleopatra's Needle on its staging platform of heavy beams. One side of its casing has been lowered to allow the photograph to be taken. Although the obelisk spent most of the last leg of its journey to Central Park encased, newspaper artists sometimes uncrated it in their drawings for dramatic effect (see below).

seemed to help, and the system had to be abandoned. Instead, a marine railway was again put into service.

The obelisk was placed lengthwise on two parallel beams joined by struts, called the cradle. Sharing the cradle was a pile-driver engine with its winch, positioned in front of the obelisk. Beams also formed the tracks, with rollers in roll boxes sandwiched between cradle and track. The anchor chain borrowed from the *Dessoug* connected a drum in the engine to a purchase block that was firmly fixed in the street ahead. The engine then hauled itself and the obelisk forward by winding the chain around the drum. Because the track extended forward, in front of the obelisk, there were extra sets of track beams and roll boxes.

Progress was slow. "The preparations for the first advance lasted until September 30th. Rainy weather, difficulty in finding suitable men, and other causes delayed the work, and the obelisk did not reach the West Boulevard [Broadway] until

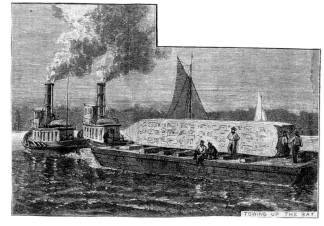

Pontoons and obelisk being towed from Staten Island, September 16, 1880. According to Gorringe, other vessels "diverged from their courses to greet the strange object with vigorous and prolonged blasts of their steam whistles and the cheers of their passengers and crews." The *Evening Telegram* (September 15, 1880) took an even more jovial tone: "A floating obelisk, it is needle-less to say, is an object of interest. Great people, the Americans! They were the first in the world to make a case for Cleopatra's needle."

October 27th." Each advance required great preparation. Gangs of men had to grade the ground ahead of the caravan, pick up the track beams from behind the obelisk, move timber and other material, reposition the beams, sink the anchors for the stationary block, and make delicate adjustments for changes in grade.

Turning the first corner was its own special torture. It took six days and nights of tedious, frustrating work to slew the obelisk southward down Broadway. With eleven turns, some as much as ninety degrees, in the route ahead, Gorringe designed an apparatus that would pivot the stone with much less fuss. It was first used eight days later at the corner of Eighty-sixth Street and Broadway. After preparing the apparatus, just four hours were needed to turn the corner.

Landing Cleopatra's Needle at Ninety-sixth Street caused a minor disruption of train service. Nothing could dampen the enthusiasm of the local newspapers, as the *New York Herald* (July 17, 1880) announced, "Cleopatra's Needle is at last in town and ready to thread some of our streets."

The obelisk and engine on the cradle beginning the laborious climb up Ninety-sixth Street. The *Evening Telegram* (September 10, 1880) reported, "The obelisk is giving some Americans a great deal more trouble than it gave the Egyptians. Cleopatra is bound to be remembered for some time to come."

All through November and December, and in the teeth of one of the coldest winters on record, Cleopatra's Needle inched along. It entered Central Park on November 25, where it faced several changes in grade and eight partial turns. "To add to the difficulties of this part of the work, intensely cold weather alternated with heavy falls of snow, and the picked men gave out one by one from attacks of rheumatism and other effects of exposure. The time occupied in moving the obelisk through the transverse road was nineteen days. Work was carried on continuously night and day by two gangs, relieving each other at six o'clock, morning and evening. I made it a point to spend six hours of each day and five hours of each night personally superintending the work."

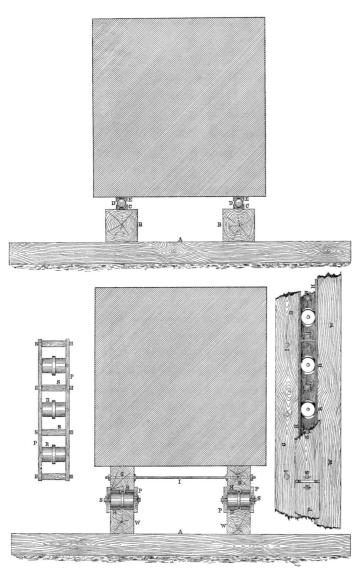

In both of these plans, heavy cross beams (A) were placed on the ground to distribute the weight evenly. In the top plan, cannonballs (D) rolled between two channels (C, E) atop track beams (B). In the bottom plan, there were track or way beams (W) and a cradle (G), on which the obelisk rode, held together by iron bolts (I) and kept apart by wooden struts (not shown). Between the cradle and track beams were roll boxes consisting of rollers (R) set between planks (P) connected by struts (S). Lengths of flat iron (H) formed grooves in track and cradle beams fitting a guide flange on the center of each roller.

Meanwhile, obelisk fever gripped the city. Crowds of curious New Yorkers gathered each day, many arriving with hammers and chisels. In fact, souvenir hunters became such a problem that a guard had to be posted around the clock to protect the stone. One entrepreneur set up a candy stand that traveled alongside the obelisk. Another confectioner sold "Cleopatra Dates" in an obelisk-shaped box that the *New York World* described as "a clever little model not only tinted in rose-color... and decorated in hieroglyphs, but capped as the original was ages ago with gold." Fashionable restaurants offered a new drink—the "Obbylish"—which was served with a needle-shaped swizzle stick and was called by the *Commercial Advertiser* an "unparalleled morning awakener."

On December 16 the obelisk arrived at Fifth Avenue and started downtown. Two days later it was at Eighty-second Street, and on December 22 it made its last turn, into the park and onto a specially built trestle. There, as it crept forward, according to a writer for the *New York Herald*, "the huge Egyptian stone was the focus of thousands of eyes. The sunshine drew out the sightseekers yesterday and the grounds south of the Metropolitan Museum of Art were black with their stovepipe hats, with occasional ribbons and bonnets diversifying the scene. All day long, their number gazed up at the obelisk."

A blizzard hit the city on December 28, and it was bitterly cold. According to Gorringe this "delayed the operation of hauling the obelisk up the trestle several days, and it did not reach its destination until January 5, 1881. On that day, the centre of gravity was placed directly over the axis of the pedestal and foundation, and its long and tedious land journey was at an end." One hundred and twelve days had passed since it had touched ground on Manhattan Island.

Cleopatra's Needle preparing to turn the corner at Eighty-sixth Street and Broadway.

ROUTE OF THE OBELISK.

Map and elevations of the route the obelisk followed in Manhattan. When Gorringe reached Central Park West, the *New York Herald* (November 30, 1880) reported that he "was to be congratulated upon the fact that the most toilsome half of the monolith's journey from the foot of West Ninety-sixth street had been made. The multitude of curiosity seekers who have followed the huge stone in its snail-paced travels ever since the evening on which it landed on Manhattan Island, now more than ten weeks ago, surrounded it yesterday when it went under arch H over the Third Transverse road [in the park]."

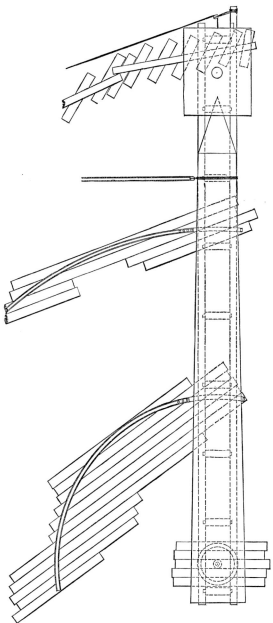

Gorringe's design for an apparatus that eased the process of turning corners with the obelisk and maneuvering around bends in the road.

Against a snowy New York background, the obelisk was an extraordinary sight crawling up the trestle to Graywacke Knoll. "Several sections of the *Dessoug*'s [heavy anchor] cable were shackled together and extended along the entire length of the trestle; one end was secured to a large steel pin that had been let into a hole drilled in the rock a short distance west of the site."

8. Installation

" . . . there arose a loud cheer which was prolonged until the shaft stood erect."

By January 20 the turning structure had been reassembled, and the trunnion plates were once more hugging the obelisk tightly around its center of gravity. Workmen had removed the trestle and all the other material spawned by the project.

That night, Gorringe and Frank Price, who had remained with the project, and five hand-picked workmen chosen for their superior skills, rendezvoused in Central Park a little before midnight. Their mission was to test the machinery by turning the obelisk.

A preview of history is a rarity, and years later Price recalled, "It was a sight always to be remembered, that immense mass in the glare of the fire light moving slowly and steadily with the power of only four men." The *New York World* reported the next day, "Bonfires had been built on each side and the scene was most weird and picturesque as the huge mass of 220 tons swung majestically from the horizontal to the vertical position. A large and merry party returning home in sleighs on the drive past the site were attracted by the fires and the sound of voices and halted to witness the experiment. They rose in their sleighs and cheered lustily as the monolith majestically rose into its position. [A half hour later,] the fires

had all been extinguished, the workmen had left for home, and the obelisk was lying horizontal again on its trunnions as if nothing had happened."

The next day a tremendous winter gale subjected the stone and machinery to another test and, according to the morning paper, "The wind had not the slightest effect on the stone, but the rain when it fell was rapidly frozen and all day the monolith looked like a huge crystal with icicles shooting from its side." The *Evening Mail* announced that, weather notwithstanding, "the Obelisk will be able to-morrow to sit up for the first time since leaving Egypt."

The official ceremony was set for noon on January 22, but as Gorringe writes, "Long before the hour fixed on for turning the obelisk, spectators had occupied every available space in the park and its vicinity from which a good view could be obtained. In spite of the piercing cold wind and thick bed of snow that lay on the ground, ladies formed at least half of the ten thousand persons estimated as the number who witnessed the operation . . . .

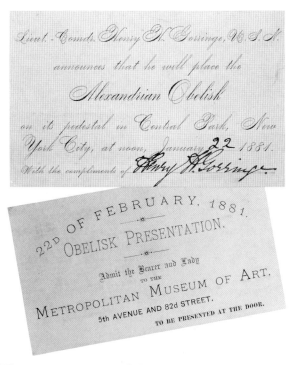

The announcement of the installation and an admission ticket to the presentation ceremonies.

"All the sleighing parties that glided up and down the Eastern Drive paused to look upon the monster overhead, and several omnibus loads of schoolboys and schoolgirls out sleighing heartily cheered the stone, creeping, imperceptibly creeping, up the inclined tramway forty-two feet above their heads" (*New York Herald*, January 4, 1881).

By January 15, 1881, the obelisk rested in a horizontal position in Gorringe's turning structure. A winter storm the night of January 21, 1881, prompted the next day's *New York Herald* to remark, "Were the obelisk anything but the solid hearted veteran that it is, yesterday's weather would have frightened it out of the idea of setting itself up in business in this country."

"A few minutes before noon the Hon. Wm. M. Evarts, Secretary of State, the Honorable Nathan Goff, Secretary of the Navy, and Mr. William Henry Hurlbert, Editor of the *New York World*, drove up to the foot of Graywacke Knoll, dismounted, and took positions reserved for them on the platform. The men stationed [at the tackles] had been previously instructed to haul down and slack away, respectively, when I held my hand up, and as long as it was held up, and to stop as soon as I lowered my hand. After a moment's conversation with Mr. Evarts the signal was given, and the obelisk slowly turned, the spectators preserving a silence that was almost unnatural. When the obelisk had changed from the horizontal to an angle of about forty-five degrees, I gave the signal to hold it in that position while Mr. Edward Bierstadt made a photograph for which he had made preparations. This seemed to break the spell that bound the spectators in silence, and when the signal was given to continue the turning there arose a loud cheer which was prolonged until the shaft stood erect. It is something to have witnessed the manipulation of a mass weighing nearly two hundred and twenty tons changing its position majestically, yet as easily and steadily as if it were without weight. It was to me an inexpressible relief to feel that my work was complete, and that no accident or incident had happened that would make my countrymen regret that

Turning the obelisk, January 22, 1881. At Gorringe's signal, the obelisk moved "as easily and delicately as if it were the minute-hand of a lady's watch. . . . Two hundred and nineteen and a quarter tons of stone, distributed in a length of sixty-nine feet two inches, are not turned in mid-air every day. As the heel of the great stone, pulled upon through reeves and blocks by half a dozen sturdy workmen, began to descend, the spectators, who crowded one another in the winter snow, and stood many rows deep behind the marines and sailor-boys, sent up cheer after cheer" (*Harper's Weekly*, February 12, 1881).

The presentation ceremony was held inside the Metropolitan Museum on February 22, 1881. It was by invitation only, but that did not stop thousands of New Yorkers from crowding the entrance, hoping to be admitted and causing pandemonium in the process.

I had been intrusted with the work of removing and re-erecting in their metropolis one of the most famous monuments of the Old World. . . . Only five minutes elapsed from the first signal to the time the obelisk was vertical. As it reached this position the Marine Band played the national airs while the battalion presented arms. Congratulations followed, and the spectators very soon dispersed."

By eight o'clock that evening, Cleopatra's Needle was resting upright on its pedestal. It had been fifteen months since the work began in Alexandria. Over the next ten days the machinery and other equipment and debris were removed from the grounds. Four newly cast bronze crabs, each weighing an average 922 pounds, had been made by Navy metalworkers in the Brooklyn Navy Yard. Each new crab bears an inscription relating to the history of the obelisk or the participants in Gorringe's tale.

"Placing and securing the crabs in position was a tedious process," writes Gorringe, "owing to continued freezing weather, and occupied us ten days longer. To give the upper part of the metal a uniform bearing, molten lead was poured into the vacant spaces and caulked in around the edges. To render their removal impossible without destroying the pedestal, molten lead was poured into the mortices around the dowels projecting downward from the lower side of the flanges, through holes bored in them for the purpose. The crabs are not ornaments only; they serve to give the bottom of the obelisk a bearing surface on the pedestal nearly equal to the area of its base if the corners had not been broken off. To pull the obelisk over without first raising it clear of the pedestal would require a force applied to its centre of gravity equivalent to that required for lifting seventy-eight tons. The maximum pressure that could be exerted by wind blowing with the force of a hurricane on the obelisk would be equivalent to that required to lift fifteen tons. . . . It would require an exceptionally severe earthquake, one that would leave very few buildings in New York standing, to render the obelisk unstable."

On February 22, 1881, Cleopatra's Needle was given an official reception a short distance away, in the Great Hall of the Metropolitan Museum, and again a huge crowd was on hand. Speeches, prayers, and hymns were intoned. Finally, commemorative bronze medals were presented to each of one hundred honor students plucked from the city's public schools. In

A gold version of the medal given to New York schoolchildren was presented to Gorringe on March 4, 1881. Both sides of the medallion are shown in the engraving opposite.

true Victorian fashion, they bear a motto that is as much an admonition as an inspiration, perhaps reflecting the trials and tribulations woven into the story of how Cleopatra's Needle came to New York:

Discipulus est priori posterior dies
(Let the future profit by lessons of the past).

Epilogue

*I am standing, Egypt, standing on my tottering
    base of stone,
As a relic of the ancient past, alas! I stand alone;
Yet I reach beyond this hemisphere, three thousand
    years and more,
Pointing backward, thro' those centuries, to the
    halcyon days of yore.*

"The Central Park Obelisk"
Charles William Darling, 1887

The summer after the obelisk came to New York, the mummy of its original owner, Thutmosis III, was found in a secret burial chamber in Egypt. He was cached in a cave high in a cliff along with some forty other pharaohs and royal personages. It was a glorious find, one that had been supporting a local family of tomb robbers for a decade. To protect the treasure from further looting, the tomb was cleared in a record six days, its contents loaded on a barge and floated down the Nile to the museum at Cairo. About this journey, Howard Carter writes, "It is a familiar story, but worth repeating, that as the barge made its way down the river, the men of the neighbouring villages fired guns for a funeral, while the women followed along the bank, tearing their hair, and uttering that shrill quavering cry of mourning for the dead, a cry that has doubtless come right down from the days of the Pharaohs themselves."

Thus, the same year that Thutmosis's obelisk settled into a new home in America, the pharaoh himself found a new resting place. Most of the other participants in the story of Cleopatra's Needle likewise went on to new ventures.

Lieutenant-Commander Henry Honeychurch Gorringe resigned from the Navy in 1883 and became a partner in the American Shipbuilding Company in Philadelphia. He published his book on obelisks and gave many lectures on his experiences. He died in 1885, at the age of forty-four, as the result of a freak accident. The newspapers give conflicting accounts of the incident, but the one most likely to be true is that succinctly given by Gorringe's old comrade, Seaton Schroeder: "Attempting to board a train in motion, he slipped and fell, receiving a fatal injury." He is buried in Rockland Cemetery, near Nyack, New York, overlooking the Hudson River, an obelisk-shaped monument marking his grave.

Seaton Schroeder remained in the Navy, served in the Spanish-American War, and was eventually promoted to rear admiral. He was commander of the Atlantic Fleet from 1909 to 1911. One of the last surviving officers to have received his appointment to Annapolis from President Lincoln, he died in 1922, the same year his memoirs were published.

The New York Obelisk, 1881. With the successful completion of the project, William Henry Hurlbert wrote in his preface to Gorringe's book, "no man knows so well as I do the discouragements and difficulties through which success was won . . . from the day in August, 1879, on which Lieut.-Commander Gorringe sailed for Europe . . . his indomitable energy was confronted at every step, not only with that wholesome bracing public indifference to such undertakings which success always startles into enthusiasm, but with all the obstacles which private greed and the eternal quarantine of official imbecility could put in his way."

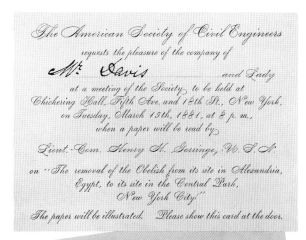

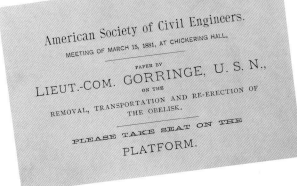

Invitation and admission ticket to one of Gorringe's lectures.

William Henry Vanderbilt went back to running his railroad, but Henry Hurlbert sold the *New York World* in 1882, its circulation having increased by the story of the obelisk. Hurlbert moved to London, where he lived for most of his remaining years. He died in Italy in 1895, the same year Ismail Pasha, the ex-khedive, died in Constantinople.

The *Dessoug*, which had served the project so well, even lending its heaviest anchor chain to the land transport, was finally granted American registry in 1881. It was sold to the Ocean Steamship Company of Savannah, Georgia, and was used first to transport cotton and then as a collier, or coal freighter. Much later, it was lost at sea.

As for Cleopatra's Needle, like many newcomers to New York, its earliest years were the most difficult. By 1885 it was showing the effects of New York's harsh winters. When a preliminary investigation turned up loose chips of stone, a flattened bullet, and colonies of microscopic plants growing in the cracks and crevices, the Parks De-

partment decided to protect the stone with a coating of paraffin, laced with creosote to prevent plant growth. A waterproofing company was hired to carry out the treatment and instructed to leave the surface intact as much as possible. Nevertheless, some 780 pounds of granite chips, flakes, scales, and fragments were removed in the process, and this may have been the greatest harm to befall the obelisk in modern times. The pieces are thought to have been taken in barrels to the American Museum of Natural History and stored in the basement. A search of the storage areas in 1983, however, turned up just a single chip, with an identifying label attached.

The paraffin, which is still present after more than a century, also caused the stone to lose its pinkish tone. The treatment did, however, help protect the obelisk's hieroglyphs from further loss, and in 1893, when isolated areas were seen to be in jeopardy, a second spot treatment of paraffin was applied. The stone was inspected again in 1913 and treated with china-wood oil, a substance then considered state of the art in museum work, but now shown to cause problems as it ages. Fortunately, the oil did not penetrate the surface and appears to have weathered away harmlessly. The most recent treatment was in 1966, when the stone was washed with a detergent.

Although Cleopatra's Needle belongs to the City of New York and is cared for by the Central Park Conservancy together with New York's Department of Parks and Recreation, the Metropolitan Museum has shown a neighborly interest in its well-being. In 1983 the Museum's Objects Conservation Department conducted a survey of the obelisk and subjected a few sample pieces to various tests to assess the true condition of the stone. They determined that the obelisk is quiescent now, no longer in active decay. Contrary to periodic reports in local newspapers, the surface has not been much harmed by the polluted atmosphere of the city, beyond being further darkened by carbon deposits and slightly roughened. Most of the apparent damage took place a long time ago in

Gorringe lectured on his adventures as well as his collection of antiquities that included part of an ancient architect's model, now in the Brooklyn Museum, for one of Heliopolis's temples.

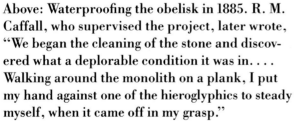

Above: Waterproofing the obelisk in 1885. R. M. Caffall, who supervised the project, later wrote, "We began the cleaning of the stone and discovered what a deplorable condition it was in. . . . Walking around the monolith on a plank, I put my hand against one of the hieroglyphics to steady myself, when it came off in my grasp."

Right (top): George Wheeler of the Metropolitan Museum's Objects Conservation Department surveying Cleopatra's Needle in 1983.

Right (bottom): Eric Young of the Museum's Egyptian department studying a report and Joseph V. Noble, then operating administrator of the Museum, inspecting the obelisk on a partial scaffolding in 1966.

Cleopatra's Needle, 1890, with the Metropolitan Museum in the background.

The Museum and the obelisk, a sweeping bird's-eye view, ca. 1928.

ancient Egypt, and it was this damage that continued to be played out when the stone first arrived in New York.

Interestingly, the tests also confirmed a piece of the obelisk's history. Using thermoluminescence, the same procedure used to date ancient pottery, they found that the stone had in fact been in a fire at exactly the time of Cambyses, when the Persians pillaged and burned ancient Heliopolis. Because the obelisk had been toppled first, part of it had been protected from the flames by the sand of the desert. The south and west faces were badly damaged, however, and are unreadable in places. Most of the loss of stone over the centuries was from this exposed area.

In addition, the toppled obelisk remained on its side, partially buried at Heliopolis for about five hundred years, until the Romans raised it in Alexandria. During this time it experienced Egypt's seasonal flooding and was further damaged by the action of salt crystallization. The salt damage made the stone more susceptible to the

effects of freeze-thaw cycles when it arrived here in 1880 and went unprotected for almost five years.

In the conclusion to their report, the Museum's scientists write, "The Obelisk is now stable, and its substance is one of the most durable of stones. It needs only the normal, routine maintenance care that such a tough, noble, irreplaceable example of an ancient culture merits." Any improvements to the stone, such as restoring it to its pinkish color, would require further study. Until such time, the safest treatment is no treatment at all.

Over the years there have been flurries of renewed interest in New York's obelisk. In 1923 its positioning relative to the compass was carefully checked. In 1932 "the strange eclipse prophesies of the obelisks" were revealed in the tabloids. Apparently, according to an anonymous source, an equally anonymous seer had erroneously predicted that the obelisks would crumble just before a solar eclipse. Occasionally, in more recent years, early morning joggers have reported seeing a mysterious group of people at sunrise encircling Cleopatra's Needle.

A handsome rail was installed around the obelisk shortly after it was settled in place, and a copper cap may have been anchored to the pyramidion at the same time. By 1966, however, the cap was gone. In 1941 a bronze plaque was attached to the rail, giving a brief history of the obelisk, and in 1956 Cecil B. deMille, who had been born in New York a few months after Cleopatra's Needle was raised in Central Park, donated four additional plaques giving translations of the hieroglyphs. De Mille included an obelisk-raising scene in his film *The Ten Commandments*, which was released the same year. He also recalled playing near the obelisk as a child. "As a boy," he said, "I used to look upon the hieroglyphs as so many wonderful pictures." In 1986 the site was relandscaped and repaved and new benches built.

The location of the obelisk has provided a topic for ongoing debate. Suggestions have been made to return the obelisk to Egypt, send it south for its health, build a glass dome over it, move it into the Museum, or at least to reposition it at the Museum's north end, to stand within view of the Temple of Dendur. Through it all, Cleopatra's Needle remains where it landed, in a quiet oasis of green. Trees and shrubbery now somewhat obscure it from the East Drive and the hordes of bicyclists, roller skaters, joggers, and cars that pass each day. Its centennial came and went almost unnoticed. The New York Freemasons restaged the foundation-laying ceremony, Governor Hugh Carey proclaimed October 4, 1980, to be Cleopatra's Needle Day, and in 1982 Lord & Taylor filled a Christmas window with a vignette of the obelisk being installed on that cold January day over a century earlier.

One of Lord & Taylor's windows, Christmas 1982. Another window vignette that year featured Metropolitan Museum staff members decorating the Main Hall in 1890.

Acknowledgments and Sources

In *A Thousand Miles Up the Nile*, Amelia Edwards observes that "to write rapidly about Egypt is impossible. The subject grows with the book, and with the knowledge one acquires by the way. . . . A date, a name, a passing reference, may cost hours of seeking." My own research in preparing this small text led me down many tangled but interesting trails and into the far recesses of some fairly daunting archives. I was given much expert guidance along the way. Staff members in departments throughout the Metropolitan Museum could not have been more helpful. I am grateful to them all, especially James Allen, Susan Allen, Dieter Arnold, and Catharine Roehrig in the Department of Egyptian Art, and George Wheeler in Objects Conservation, for their gentle corrections and generous advice. Joan Holt and Tonia Payne in the Editorial Department made many valuable suggestions and helped with numerous details.

I am indebted to the librarians, archivists, and others who helped me locate material in the Museum of the City of New York, the New-York Historical Society, the New York Public Library, the New York Society Library, and the Thomas J. Watson Library, Metropolitan Museum of Art. Thank-yous to William Moore, director, the Chancellor Robert R. Livingston Library and Museum, Masonic Hall; Jann Walker, publicity director, Lord & Taylor; Beth Dreisher, editor, *Coin World*; Jonathan Kuhn, curator, monuments, the New York Department of Parks and Recreation; and, finally, Michael Shroyer and Barbara Burn for yet another exhilarating collaboration.

Selected Bibliography

Abd al-Latif. *Relation de l'Egypte*. Paris, 1810. Cited in Budge, *Cleopatra's Needles*, p. 166.

Breasted, James Henry. "The Obelisks of Thutmose III and his Building Season in Egypt." *Zeitschrift fur aegyptische Sprache und Altertumskunde* 39 (1901), pp. 55–62.

Budge, E. A. Wallis. *Cleopatra's Needles and Other Egyptian Obelisks*. London, 1926 (repr. New York: Dover Publications, 1990).

Caffall, R. M. "An address delivered before the New York Academy of Sciences, November 23, 1885, by R. Caffall on his process for waterproofing and preserving Buildings as recently applied to the obelisk in Central Park." New York, 1886. Pamphlet. New-York Historical Society, New York.

Clarke, Somers and R. Engelbach. *Ancient Egyptian Construction and Architecture*. New York, 1990.

Denon, D. Vivant. *Travels in Upper and Lower Egypt During the Campaigns of General Bonaparte . . . .* Trans. Arthur Aiken. London, 1803.

Edwards, Amelia B. *A Thousand Miles Up the Nile*. New York, 1877.

Engelbach, Reginald. *The Problem of the Obelisks*. New York, 1923.

———. *The Aswan obelisk with some remarks on ancient engineering*. Cairo, 1922.

Farman, Elbert E. "The Negotiations for the Obelisk." *The Century* 24, New Series 2 (May–October 1882), pp. 879–89.

Flaubert, Gustave. *Flaubert in Egypt: A Sensibility on Tour*. Trans. Francis Steegmuller. Boston, 1972.

Gorringe, Henry Honeychurch. *Egyptian Obelisks*. New York, [1882].

Guren, Jay. "Obelisk Dedication Spawns Unique Gold Masonic Medal." *Coin World* (December 27, 1972), p. 30.

Habachi, Labib. *The Obelisks of Egypt: Skyscrapers of the Past*. Cairo, 1984.

Hellman, Geoffrey T. "That Was New York: A Needle for Central Park." *The New Yorker* (September 3, 1938), pp. 24–32.

Howe, Winifred Eva. *A History of the Metropolitan Museum of Art*. New York, 1913.

Johnson, Irving and Electa. *Yankee Sails the Nile*. New York, 1966.

Obélisque, dit de Cléopatre, à Alexandrie. Copper engraving by Marcus Tuscher (1705–51).

Julien, Alexis A. *Notes of Research on the New York Obelisk*. Offprint (repr. from *Bulletin of the American Geographical Society*, March 1893). New York Society Library, New York.

Lepsius, Richard. *Discoveries in Egypt, Ethiopia and the Peninsula of Sinai, in the years 1842–1845*, 2nd ed. London, 1853.

Lewin, Seymour Z., George E. Wheeler, and A. E. Charola. "Stone Conservation and Cleopatra's Needle: A Case History and an Object Lesson." Department of Objects Conservation, Metropolitan Museum of Art, New York, 1983.

Moldenke, Charles E. *The New York Obelisk: Cleopatra's Needle*. New York, 1891.

New York City Department of Parks. "Copy of Report on the Condition of the Obelisk in the Central Park, New York by a committee of experts appointed by the Department of Public Parks." New York, 1890. Pamphlet (extr. from official documents of the board).

["The obelisk"]. A scrapbook consisting of articles taken from American and English newspapers and periodicals and other memorabilia, 1879–1941. Thomas J. Watson Library, Metropolitan Museum of Art, New York.

Pliny the Elder. *Natural History*. Trans. D. E. Eichholz. Loeb Classical Library, no. 419. Cambridge, Mass., 1962.

[Price, Frank.] "Description of the Method and Machinery used in Moving Our Egyptian Obelisk, Known as Cleopatra's Needle, From Alexandria, Egypt, to Central Park, New York City." Department of Egyptian Art, Metropolitan Museum of Art, New York.

Roberts, David. *Egypt and Nubia*, vol. 1. London, 1846.

Schroeder, Seaton. *A Half Century of Naval Service*. New York, 1922.

Spon, Jacob, and George Wheeler. *Voyage d'Italie, de Dalmatie, de Grèce, et du Levant fait aux années 1675 et 1676*. Lyons, 1678.

Tirard, Helen M. B. and Nestor. *Sketches from a Nile Steamer for the Use of Travellers in Egypt*. London, 1891.

Picture Credits

Unless otherwise noted, photography by the Photograph Studio, The Metropolitan Museum of Art.

Inside front cover, pp. 2, 12 (right), 15 (left), 18 (bottom), 22 (right), 31, 33, 34 (right), 35, 36 (left), 38–40, 42, 44, 45, 47–50, 51 (bottom), 53, 58, 59, 61, 62, 64, 66, 67: from ["The Obelisk"]; pp. 3 (right), 12 (right), 16, 20, 29, 34 (right): from Tirard, *Sketches from a Nile Steamer*; p. 4: from Johnson, *Yankee Sails the Nile*; p. 5 (top): from Habachi, *The Obelisks of Egypt*; p. 5 (bottom): from Clarke, *Ancient Egyptian Construction and Architecture*; pp. 6–10, 13, 15 (right), 17 (top), 19, 21, 23–27, 30, 31, 36–37, 43, 51 (top), 52, 54–57, 60, 65, inside back cover: from Gorringe, *Egyptian Obelisks*; p. 11: from Farman, "Negotiations for the Obelisk," courtesy New York Society Library; p. 14: Department of Egyptian Art, Metropolitan Museum of Art (photo: Felix Bonfils); p. 18 (top): Hulton-Deutsch Collection, London; p. 28: The Bettmann Archive; pp. 32, 41, 68 (top left): New-York Historical Society; p. 63: *Coin World*, courtesy Chancellor Robert R. Livingston Library and Museum, Masonic Hall, New York; p. 68 (top right): Objects Conservation, Metropolitan Museum of Art; p. 68 (bottom right): New York City Parks Photo Archive; p. 69: Museum of the City of New York (photo: Adolph Witteman; Leonard Hassam Bogart Collection); p. 71: Lord & Taylor, New York; p. 72: Museum of the City of New York (Gift of Joseph Verner Reed, 50.358.19). Back cover: photo by Karen Willis, the Photograph Studio, The Metropolitan Museum of Art.

Inside front cover: William H. Forbes and Co. Lithograph. ca. 1880–1900. 17¾ x 13¾ in. (45.1 x 34.9 cm)

P. 3: Fragmentary relief, limestone with touches of color. Dynasty 18. 12⅝ x 12⅝ in. (32 x 32 cm)

P. 17: Engraving. 20½ x 45⅟₁₆ in.

P. 23: Support crab, bronze. Roman period. h. 7⅞ in. (20 cm); w. 23⅝ in. (60 cm)